CHEROKEE

people of the written word

CHEROKEE

people of the written word

Wayne Youngblood

CHARTWELL
BOOKS, INC.

This edition published in 2008 by

CHARTWELL BOOKS, INC.
A Division of
BOOK SALES, INC.
114 Northfield Avenue
Edison, New Jersey 08837

ISBN 13: 978-0-7858-2398-8
ISBN 10: 0-7858-2398-0

© 2008 Compendium Publishing Ltd
43 Frith Street, London, Soho, W1D 4SA

Design: Compendium Design/Donald Sommerville

Mapping: Mark Franklin

Printed and bound in China

Thanks to Bo Taylor of the Museum of the Cherokee Indian who supplied most of the iomages in this book. All uncredited images are from the author's collection.

PAGE 1: Black Coat or Tehkenehkee, a Western Cherokee chief, one of several versions of the painting by George Catlin from his initial study made at Fort Gibson in 1834.

PAGE 2: "Tuch-ee, a Cherokee War Chief" from a painting by George Catlin in Dr Prichard's *Natural History of Man*. *The Art Archive/Buffalo Bill Historical Center, Cody, Wyoming*.

RIGHT: The Wolfetown Ball Game team, 1887. *Museum of the Cherokee Indian*

Contents

Introduction

"Our hearts are sickened . . ." John Ross, 1836

For those American Indians raised on reservations or strongly affiliated with tribes for more than one generation, it's normal to be Indian, with all the struggles and rewards associated with the various tribal cultures. The identities of these people are clear.

But there is another modern Indian face, one that is no less Indian than those on the reservation, but not recognized as such. A number of us are American Indian by blood, but not necessarily by culture. We have a significant percentage of Indian ancestry, but are not registered or actively involved with tribal life. As a result, we neither reap the benefits (financial or cultural) nor the heartaches (financial or cultural) of being identified as Indian. We're considered white by many Indians and Indian by many whites—a theme identified and made popular by Cherokee pop singer Cher's song, "Half Breed." This is also the case for many Cherokee, who

are part of the largest—if not most divided and splintered—American Indian tribe.

Being Cherokee cannot be defined by a single concept. It is a completely different experience for those living in the Eastern Band in North Carolina, the Keetoowah Band and Cherokee Nation in Oklahoma, and for those affiliated and non-affiliated Cherokee living all over the United States and in many other countries.

Benito Pablo Juárez García, the first and only full-blood Indian (a Zapotec) to serve as president of Mexico, made the following statement to Emperor Maximilian in 1864:

"It is given to men, Sir, to attack the rights of others, to take their property, to attempt the lives of those who defend their liberty, and to make of their virtues a crime and their vices a virtue; but there is one thing which is beyond the reach of perversity, and that is the tremendous verdict of history. History will judge us."

Even though Juárez García had nothing to do with the Cherokee or the many injustices done to them, he might just as well have been speaking directly of the tribe. The betrayal of the Cherokee—the tribe that reached a higher peak of Western civilization than any other North American Indian tribe—began early and was often at the hands of whites whom the tribe originally counted as friends. These individuals include American icons Thomas

Oklahoma Indian Centennial stamp. In 1948, the United States Post Office released a stamp to mark the centennial of the Trail of Tears (ten years too late). It features the seals of the "Five Civilized Tribes." *WilshireImages/ iStockphoto*

In 1730, Alexander Cuming took seven Cherokee men to England in an effort to secure Cherokee loyalty. The seven are shown here in St. James Gardens, London, wearing clothes given to them by King George II. Oconostota is third from left, and Attakullakulla is the figure at far right.

Jefferson and Andrew Jackson. Jefferson devised a scheme whereby the Cherokee were given unlimited credit at trading posts in an effort to get them so deeply indebted they would have to continue giving up land to the whites. Jackson, who counted on the help of the Cherokee to fight the Creek and by at least one account owed his life to them, very openly betrayed the tribe in events leading up to the Removal Act of 1830 and their forced removal to what is now Oklahoma in 1838–39. The unilateral Indian Removal Act Jackson penned stated that Indians must give up all land east of the Mississippi in exchange for land out west. Those who chose not to move were supposed to be made citizens of

whatever state in which they lived, but with absolutely no title to their land.

Many historians seem to equate the entire Cherokee story with the descendants who now live in Oklahoma, following the story in the eastern United States through the 1838–39 Trail of Tears (forced removal), then shifting entirely to a western focus. But some of the Cherokee—about 1,000—were not captured and removed from their homes. Some were made citizens of the United States, others hid in the hills of their native lands, eventually purchasing land, being recognized by the government and forming the Eastern Band. The Eastern Band, which is considerably smaller than the Cherokee Nation and

A lone fisherman ventures out on an early, misty morning on Cherokee Lake, Tennessee. Cherokee Lake is located in the heart of ancestral Cherokee territory, *c.* 1990s. *Richard Hamilton Smith, Corbis*

about equal in size to the Keetoowah Band, should not be ignored. They represent the mother stock of the entire Cherokee people. Now, still living on their ancestral lands, the North Carolina Cherokee on the Qualla Boundary Reservation still play the ancient game of Indian Ball, compete in blowgun and bowmanship contests, participate in other ceremonies, and engage in activities that were begun centuries before the European invasion. They lead relatively quiet lives and focus on betterment of their families and tribe. To gain some perspective on those Cherokee who remain on ancestral lands, I visited the North Carolina reservation.

Passing boarded-up tourist traps and boiled peanut stands as I descended through the steep mountainous terrain on narrow, tree-lined and winding Highway 19 into the town of Cherokee, I was struck by several things. On that cold winter morning I was headed to meet with the archivist of the Museum of the Cherokee Indian to locate many of the photos you see in this book. Cherokee, which borders the Great Smoky Mountains, is located on the southwestern edge of the comparatively tiny parcel of land in North Carolina that is now all that remains of the vast ancestral lands of the Cherokee. That area, which once covered more than 40,000 square miles, now includes the reservation—an area that comprises only about 88 square miles of land.

As I neared the reservation I was first struck by the natural beauty of the land. True, modern men, both Anglo and Indian, have done what they could to place their marks on the land, scarring it deeply—and the town itself is very much a tourist destination (at least in part out of financial necessity)—but the mountains are alive with their natural beauty. How truly heartbreaking it must have been for those who were forced to relocate to Oklahoma to be hauled forcibly from their ancestral homes—homes with the easy familiarity and striking beauty of the mountains, trees, and streams known by many generations past—to a land comparatively devoid of landscape. Yet this anguish must have been at least somewhat eased for those who survived, by the knowledge that they survived. Estimates are that more than a quarter of the 16,000 or so who marched died along the way. Nonetheless, the Cherokee proved themselves to be hardy stock and quite willing to take on the challenges of surviving and scratching out a living in a totally unfamiliar land. Those who moved west have done well.

I also was struck by the fact that in the 21st century the Cherokee remain a deeply divided people. Despite the fact that they form the largest existing tribe of North American Indians, Cherokee history is full of splits, rifts, and missteps, with at least three main recognized groups that have little inter-tribal cooperation still in existence. These include the Eastern Band (the mother stock of all Cherokee), the Old Settlers (now usually known as the Keetoowah Band) and the Oklahoma Cherokee, the descendants of those forced west by American treachery and expansion more than 170 years ago. Tens of thousands of other Cherokee—both recognized and not—live all over the United States and in other countries. Although there is some cooperation between the Eastern Band and the Cherokee Nation, the Keetoowah Band pretty well keeps to itself.

Today, the town of Cherokee, N.C., reflects much of modern American Indian society, as well as contemporary American culture in general. There is a massive Harrah's casino in town, dwarfing the inevitable accompanying string of hotels, fast-food restaurants and tourist traps. There also are a number of billboards promoting diabetes prevention, spouse abuse intervention, religion, and literacy. But get off the beaten path a bit and there's also a great sense of

quiet peace that trickles through the hills like the Oconaluftee River. The tourist traps, by the way, are not new. They've been around for decades as a pre-casino means of raising desperately needed revenue for members of the tribe and other area residents. Before it became chic to be Indian, attractions such as Santa's Land (complete with the "Rudicoaster") and the Smoky Mountain Gold Ruby Mine dotted the land, along with Indian "curio" stands. Although these still exist, they've been overshadowed by Harrah's, the Oconaluftee Indian Village, a moccasin outlet, an outdoor theatre featuring the story of the Cherokee ("Unto These Hills"), and the museum itself. But there is much more to the story of the Cherokee Indian.

Cherokee legend holds that the Cherokee people have always lived in what is now the southeastern United States. Archeological evidence suggests that they have lived there more than 10,000 years. Either way, the Cherokee people were residents of the area long before Europeans had any contact with them.

In terms of recorded history, whatever you may or may not know about the Cherokee, it is likely you are at least familiar with the Trail of Tears—the forced removal of the Cherokee people in 1838–39, a primarily winter journey that covered four routes (three land and one water) and resulted in the deaths of more than 4,000 of the 16,000 or so who were forced to move. It is this event—and a thousand smaller events leading up to it—that essentially cleaves the history of the Cherokee in two: before the Treaty of New Echota and after.

It is perhaps most ironic that the bitterest chapter of Cherokee history—their forced removal from ancestral lands—is what likely preserved the Cherokee and much of their culture from the fate that befell most Indian tribes. If Major Ridge, his

A large wooden statue of Sequoyah stands at the entrance to the Museum of the Cherokee Indian in Cherokee, North Carolina. It was sculpted by Peter Wolf Toth from a single Sequoia redwood log. *The Art Archive/Global Book Publishing*

Bo Taylor, lifetime Eastern Band tribal member and archivist with the Museum of the Cherokee Indian is also known as a dancer. He is pictured here during the 1980s. *Museum of the Cherokee Indian*

nephew, Elias Boudinot, and others had never signed the Treaty of New Echota on December 29, 1835, the Cherokee likely would have made a stand against the whites to preserve their land—a stand that would almost certainly have resulted in the mass butchering of many people, the eventual near-total absorption of the Cherokee into American society, and would not have likely changed the eventual outcome in terms of land ownership anyway. The white man was technologically and numerically superior to the Cherokee and was determined to have their land. Indeed, Boudinot recognized this when he wrote in 1837, "If one hundred persons are ignorant of their true situation, and are so completely blinded as not to see the destruction that awaits them, we can see strong reasons to justify the actions of a minority of fifty persons to do what the majority would do if they understood their condition—to save a nation from political thralldom and moral degradation."

Ridge, like Boudinot, knew this, and explained his decision to the Americans: "I am one of the native sons of these wild woods. I have hunted the deer and turkey here, more than fifty years. I have fought your battles [a reference to the times the Cherokee were asked by the American government to fight against other tribes to preserve white interests]." Speaking of the land, Ridge continued, "I know the Indians have an older title . . . we obtained the land from the living God above." Despite this, he knew resistance was useless. "We are few, they are many. We cannot stay here in safety and comfort." Speaking of the struggle for native lands, Ridge stated that "I would willingly die to preserve them, but any forcible effort to keep them will cost us our lands, our lives, and the lives of our children."

Ridge's decision did indeed cost him his life. He was assassinated, along with his son, John, and Boudinot on July 12, 1839, during the summer after removal to Oklahoma, for their parts in signing the Treaty of New Echota. Within three weeks of the brutal killing of these three, the Cherokee Council declared that because the men had signed the treaty they were outlaws and that their murders were legal executions. The same session also declared the Treaty of New Echota null and void.

The Cherokee people, called one of the "Five Civilized Tribes" (with the Choctaw, Chickasaw, Muscogee, and Seminole), are among the oldest settlers in what is now North America. These once inhabited a vast area of about 40,000 square miles, and had about 60 villages, connected to each other and the outside world by seven main groups of trails. Echota, a settlement on the south bank of the Little Tennessee River, seems to have been considered the capital of the nation.

Early Cherokee dwellings were built of poles covered inside and out with interwoven twigs or mixed clay and grass, and some structures housed several families. However, by the 18th century, Cherokees had largely adopted the log cabin styles of white frontier settlers, along with other European material and social influences. The Cherokee, unlike most other American Indian tribes, embraced white culture and "civilization," which was as much a curse as it was a blessing.

For the first 200 years of contact, the Cherokees generally extended hospitality and help to the newcomers. Peaceful trade prevailed, with only a few hostile outbursts (generally provoked), and intermarriage was not uncommon. The Cherokees were quick to embrace useful aspects of the newcomers' culture, from tools and implements to strange new fruits and vegetables.

The Cherokee also saw the usefulness of a written language, something that had not previously existed for them. This was created by half-Cherokee genius Sequoyah, who was born about 1771. His mother was Cherokee and his father was a white trader. Sequoyah never went to school, nor did he ever learn to read or write English, yet he introduced his "syllabary" to the national council in 1821. The Cherokee syllabary is composed of 86 characters, each representing a syllable (rather than letter) of the

Cherokee language, thus the name. Within a few months, the majority of the Cherokee nation learned this written language and became "literate." But this was not enough. The encroaching Europeans wanted the Indians off the land.

Although the Trail of Tears is known as a specific event that occurred over the winter of 1838–39, there was much that led up to it. A long series of broken promises and treaties preceded the event, including a total of 36 incidents between 1785 and 1835, in which the Cherokee were forced to give up more land. The first treaty made with the Cherokee (and the first one broken), was the 1785 Treaty of Hopewell, whereby a specific border of Cherokee territory was established, and whereby only Indians were allowed to settle within it. Only five years later, more than 500 white families had built settlements on Cherokee land. President Washington asked Congress to intervene, but Congress instead drew up a new treaty.

In 1791, the Treaty of Holston was signed. This treaty called for the Cherokee to give up the lands already taken by the whites in exchange for $1,000 per year (it was increased to $1,500 per year in 1792). The treaty also called for new territorial borders, with the promise that Cherokee land would be protected from all intruders by the full strength of the American government. The treaty also stated that friendly relations between the Cherokee and the Americans would be "permanent" and "perpetual." The treaty, however, neither stopped the surge of white settlers, nor did it result in any action on the part of the American government.

More treaties were drawn up in 1794 and 1798, each time requiring the Cherokees to give up more land, with the promise they would be protected. The Tellico Treaty of 1798—signed just 40 years before the forced relocation—even went so

ABOVE: An inscribed silver gorget that belonged to Ostenaco, who earned the title "Outacite" (meaning "Man-Killer") for his great bravery on the battlefield. It was given to him July 8, 1762, by Britain's King George III. *Museum of the Cherokee Indian*

OPPOSITE: Satirical verses about the arrival in London of three Cherokee chiefs on an embassy to the Court of George III. *Library of Congress, LC-USZ62-102370*

had already been signed, and Georgia expected to be able to take possession of the land.

Further complicating matters and intensifying the struggle was a gold rush that manifested itself near Dahlonega, Georgia, which lies in the northern part of the state, within 50 miles of the borders of Tennessee and both North and South Carolina (fewer than 100 miles from the current Qualla Reservation).

In 1799, 12-year-old Conrad Reed found a 17-pound gold nugget on his father's farm, near Cabarrus, N.C. (east of present-day Charlotte). In 1802, the family sold the nugget to a jeweler for $3.50, and the news touched off a gold rush in the area, with gold seekers trespassing on much Cherokee land. From there, gold was found along what became known as the Appalachian Gold Belt (mostly on Cherokee land), culminating with a major strike in 1828, near Dahlonega. The name comes from the Cherokee language for "yellow money."

In 1813, the "Red Stick" Creeks (named for the color of their war clubs) vowed to kill all white settlers. They began by attacking Fort Mims (in Alabama), killing more than 250 people. Andrew Jackson was assigned to put this uprising down, and enlisted the aid of friendly Creeks and more than 500 Cherokee to do so.

After the Battle of Horseshoe Bend, which effectively ended the uprising (where Cherokee Junaluska supposedly saved Jackson's life), the Cherokee and Creek were incredulous at the terms of surrender. Jackson called for the Creek to give up 23 million acres of land as a condition of peace (fully half of the entire tribal land holdings). Only a relatively small number of Creeks had gone to war, with the rest aiding Jackson. Also, the Cherokee felt they owned about four million of these acres, and

far as to specify that the Cherokee would never have to leave their land.

In 1802, Thomas Jefferson mad a bold, if not illegal, move. He signed the "Deed of Articles and Mutual Cession" with Georgia, in which Georgia was to give up land to the United States (which became much of Alabama and Mississippi), in exchange for all land contained within the present-day borders of Georgia. Most of that land belonged to the Cherokee, and Jefferson knew it. He perhaps intended to purchase the land from the Cherokee, but that was not how it worked out. The Cherokee did not wish to sell, but the compact with Georgia

there was other land in this huge parcel that was disputed by other tribes. For their part the Creek had little choice but to sign.

Hoping once again that the government might help, the Cherokee went to President James Madison, asking him to intervene. Madison in turn directed Jackson to try to purchase the disputed land through more treaties if possible. Jackson was outraged, feeling he had won the land and did not need to negotiate further.

Eventually, he and nine Cherokee chiefs met and signed the Treaty of Turkey Town in 1816, which called for the "purchase" of about 1.3 million acres by the United States. About 4,000 Cherokee gave up their eastern lands in exchange for land in northwest Arkansas. This group formed the basis of what would eventually be recognized as the Western Cherokee (now Keetoowah). This treaty also set another precedent. Language in the treaty stated it was "ratified at Turkey Town by the whole Cherokee Nation," when in fact only nine chiefs signed. This tactic was used other times, including in the Treaty of New Echota, to represent small tricked, bribed, or frightened groups as the "whole Cherokee Nation."

Despite calling himself "Friend and Brother" of the Indians, Jackson wanted to be completely rid of them by whatever means it took. His writings expose that he felt, among other things, that Indians were inferior to European settlers and that they posed a probable security threat to the young nation.

Among the excuses used for relocating the Cherokee was that the Indians were not using their land efficiently and that it should be given to white farmers. But much evidence suggests that the highly adaptive Cherokee were learning European farming methods with a great deal of success. Many now lived in European-style homes and dressed in modern clothing. To help demonstrate that the Cherokee

A NEW HUMOROUS SONG,
ON THE
CHEROKEE CHIEFS.
Inscribed to the LADIES of GREAT BRITAIN.
By H. HOWARD.

To the Tune of, *Cæsar and Pompey were both of them Horned.*

I.

WHAT a Piece of Work's here, and a d——d Botheration !
Of Three famous Chiefs from the *Cherokee* Nation ;
Who the Duce wou'd ha' thought, that a People polite, Sir,
Wou'd ha' stir'd out o' Doors to ha' seen such a Sight, Sir ?
Are M——rs so rare in the *British* Dominions,
That we thus shou'd run crazy for *Canada Indians.*
Are M——rs so rare, &c.

II.

How eager the Folks at *Vauxhall,* or elsewhere, Sir,
With high Expectation and Rapture repair, Sir ;
Tho' not one of them all can produce the least Reason,
Save that M——rs of all Sorts are always in Season.
If so, let the Chiefs here awhile have their Station,
And send for the whole of the *Cherokee* Nation.
If so, let the Chiefs, &c.

III.

The Ladies, dear Creatures, so squeamish and dainty,
Surround the great *Canada* Warriors in plenty ;
Wives, Widows and *Matrons,* and pert little *Misses,*
Are pressing and squeezing for *Cherokee* Kisses.
Each grave looking Prude, and each smart looking Belle, Sir,
Declaring, no *Englishman* e'er kiss'd so well, Sir.
Each grave looking Prude, &c.

IV.

That *Cherokee* Lips are much softer and sweeter,
Their Touch more refin'd, and their Kisses repleter ;
The fair ones agree——nay, I mean not to flatter,
For who like the Ladies can judge of the Matter ?
Ye Nymphs then, who like 'm, indulge your odd Passion,
Be sw——d by the Chiefs of the *Cherokee* Nation.
Ye Nymphs then, &c.

V.

Ye Females of *Britain,* so wanton and witty,
Who love even Monkies, and swear they are pretty ;
The *Cherokee* Indians, and stranger *Shimpanzeys,*
By Turns, pretty Creatures, have tickl'd your Fancies ;
Which proves, that the Ladies so fond are of Billing,
They'd kiss even M——rs, were M——rs as willing.
Which proves, that, &c.

VI.

No more then these Chiefs, with their scalping Knives dread, Sir,
Shall strip down the Skin from the *Englishman's* Head, Sir ;
Let the Case be revers'd, and the Ladies prevail, Sir,
And instead of the Head, skin the *Cherokee* T——l, Sir.
Ye bold Female *Scalpers,* courageous and hearty,
Collect all your Force for a *grand Scalping Party.*
Ye bold Female Scalpers, &c.

VII.

For Weapons, ye Fair, you've no need to petition,
No Weapons you'll want for this odd Expedition ;
A soft Female Hand, the best Weapon I wean is,
To strip down the Bark of a *Cherokee P——s.*
Courageous advance then, each fair *English* Tartar,
Scalp the *Chiefs* of the *Scalpers,* and give them no Quarter.
Courageous advance then, &c.

Sold by the AUTHOR, opposite the Union Coffee-House, in the Strand, near Temple-Bar, and by all the Print and Pamphlet-sellers.
[PRICE SIX-PENCE.]
N. B. In a few Days will be published the *Political Bagpiper.* A new Song, with a Head-piece.

(Major) Ridge, "Kahmungdaclageh." Lithograph after a painting by George Bird King in McKenney and Hall's *History of the Indian Tribes of North America*. Ridge (as his shortened surname became), was born about 1771. He attained the rank of major during the Creek War. At the signing of the Treaty of New Echota, Ridge believed that removal was the only way his people would survive. He was later murdered as a traitor. *Author's collection*

were sovereign and not inferiors needing protection, they drew up a constitution in 1827 and elected John Ross principal chief. But Georgia continued to push for removal and the previously mentioned gold rush of 1828 only made things worse.

Between 1828 and 1830, Georgia nullified all Cherokee law, stated the Indians were subject to its laws, and forbade them to enforce their own laws or hold trials. Further, Cherokees could not even testify in any Georgia court. Lotteries were held for the Cherokee land. Settlers' names were drawn from a drum to let them know where their "new" land was located, and they were entitled to the land and anything on it, including homes and other buildings. Many Cherokee families found that their first notification of this was when settlers showed up to

John Ross or Guwisguwi. From a lithograph, in McKenney and Hall. John Ross was only one-eighth blood Cherokee. He was the son of a Scottish immigrant and a Cherokee woman who was a quarter-blood. He was born in 1790 and died in Washington in 1866. *Art Archive/Buffalo Bill Historical Center*

take possession, usually by force. Since Andrew Jackson was now president, the Cherokees realized that appealing to the president would no longer produce any result.

In 1831, the Cherokee did, however, appeal to the U.S. Supreme Court, asking for an injunction to prevent Georgia from following through with all its plans (*Cherokee Nation vs. Georgia*). Chief Justice John Marshall found that the Cherokee were wards of the United States and, as such, had no right to sue in federal court. The Cherokee now neither had their sovereignty acknowledged, nor did they get the injunction. However, the following year, Marshall found that the Cherokee formed a "distinct community" under U.S. protection (*Worcester vs. Georgia*). That meant that Georgia law had no

The Oklahoma Cherokee

The Cherokee in Oklahoma are split into two self-governing groups: the Western Cherokee and the Cherokee Nation. The Western Cherokee are the descendants of a number of conservatives who moved west years ahead of the main body, as well as those who were supporters of the so-called Treaty Party that negotiated the Treaty of New Echota. The Cherokee Nation includes descendants of what were the most acculturated (to white culture) members of the tribe, operating schools, newspapers and churches, as well as owning black slaves.

bearing on Cherokee land, and that all the new rulings regarding the Cherokee, their laws, and their land were not valid. It was a hollow victory. President Jackson not only did not perform his presidential duty of upholding the court's decision, he openly defied the Supreme Court.

"In truth, our cause is your own," began John Ross in a September 28, 1836, letter to the Senate and House of Representatives, protesting the Treaty of New Echota. "It is the cause of liberty and of justice. It is based upon your own principles, which we have learned from yourselves; for we have gloried to count your Washington and your Jefferson our great teachers. We have read their communications to us with veneration; we have practised their precepts with success. And the result is manifest. The wildness of the forest has given place to comfortable dwellings and cultivated fields, stocked with the various domestic animals. Mental culture, industrious habits, and domestic enjoyments, have succeeded the rudeness of the savage state.

"We have learned your religion also. We have read your Sacred books. Hundreds of our people have embraced their doctrines, practised the virtues they teach, cherished the hopes they awaken, and rejoiced in the consolations which they afford . . . But we speak to the representatives of a Christian country; the friends of justice; the patrons of the oppressed. And our hopes revive, and our prospects brighten, as we indulge the thought. On your sentence, our fate is suspended; prosperity or desolation depends on your word. To you, therefore, we look! Before your august assembly we present ourselves, in the attitude of deprecation, and of entreaty. On your kindness, on your humanity, on your compassion, on your benevolence, we rest our hopes. To you we address our reiterated prayers. Spare our people! Spare the wreck of our prosperity! Let not our deserted homes become the monuments of our desolation!"

Ross continued to plead with the U.S. government until after removal had begun.

By 1838, the U.S. government was no longer even attempting to put forward false treaties and offers of friendship. The Treaty of New Echota had been signed two years earlier and Jackson was determined to follow through. The choice of the Cherokee was now simple: move or be moved. Forts that would serve as temporary removal prisons had been under construction since five months after the 1830 Indian Removal Act was signed, and served as daily reminders to the Cherokee of what was to come.

When the steamroller of forced removal finally came in May 1838, it was swift and terrifying. About 7,000 regular troops, under the command of General Winfield Scott, came to every doorstep of every Cherokee town and within about two weeks forced the residents out at bayonet point, pushing them to the temporary camps. If they were foolish enough to resist they were frequently beaten with rifle butts and other weapons. This treatment was, however, against Scott's wishes. He issued specific commands to treat the Indians with dignity, respect, and kindness. The Georgia Guard had other ideas.

Although some Cherokee headed west within a few weeks, most were held from four to six months. The temporary forts were never intended to hold so many people for so long. Close quarters and grossly insufficient sanitary provisions led to rampant disease. Hundreds of Cherokee died before they even embarked on the Trail of Tears. Further complicating matters were the guards, who sold food that was supposed to go to the Indians to local settlers.

In all, there were ten different routes (variations of four primary ones) that are now known collectively as the "Trail of Tears." Three groups of Cherokee totaling about 2,800 were sent out west in June 1838. That summer was extremely hot, and drought caused many of the rivers to run significantly lower than normal. Boats got hung up on sandbars, forcing overcrowding in those that did not. This resulted in still more illness and death.

The 13 remaining groups back east were held up until much later, in hopes the weather would be cooler and the drought would break. Those groups left from October through December, but an early and colder than normal winter froze the rivers and forced more overland walking. Many of the Indians had no blankets or shoes.

Most Americans were fully unaware of what their government had done. Indeed, President Martin Van Buren, in an address to Congress on

A group of Cherokee are shown fishing in a stream on the Qualla Boundary Reservation. By working as a group in a line, the catch is larger. *c. 1890s. Museum of the Cherokee Indian*

The Eastern Band

A number of Cherokee—about 1,000—escaped forced removal. In 1889, a reservation was formally established around a number of communities near the Great Smoky Mountains in North Carolina. This is known as the Qualla Reservation of the Eastern Cherokees. Until recently, the Eastern Cherokee were a more conservative group than those in the Cherokee Nation. They have retained the Ball Game (played with two sticks to catch the ball, and attempt to get it through a goal) and other old games. They have dances and basketry at their annual Cherokee Indian Fair, and the tribe operates a reconstructed "Oconaluftee Indian Village" and the Museum of the Cherokee Indian. Both Eastern and Western Cherokee also operate outdoor dramas, called Unto These Hills, in an attempt to show their own version of Cherokee history.

OPPOSITE: Eastern Cherokee man and woman preparing and making cane baskets, Qualla Reservation, North Carolina, c. 1950. Cherokee baskets are still made from white oak, river cane and recently honeysuckle, and various dyeing and decorating materials. Cane is split into splints, then peeled and trimmed, and finally plaited into a variety of basket shapes using wickerwork, checkerwork and twilling techniques. *Postcard of Oconaluftee Indian village, Cherokee Historical Association*

December 8, 1838 (while hundreds of Cherokee were still dying in miserable conditions), stated that "It affords me great pleasure to apprise the Congress of the entire removal of the Cherokee Nation of Indians to their new homes west of the Mississippi. The measures authorized by Congress at its last session have had the happiest effects . . ." He went on to state that much of the removal was supervised by "their own chiefs, and they have migrated without apparent reluctance."

A white traveler who spent three days with a group under Rev. Jesse Bushyhead, had a different opinion, as he watched women and children die from trudging along, starving and with bleeding feet. "When I passed the last detachment of these suffering exiles and thought that my countrymen expelled them from their native soil and their beloved homes," he wrote, "I turned from the sight with feelings which language cannot express, and wept like a child."

The final detachment of Cherokee survivors arrived in Indian Territory on March 26, 1839. One of those who did not complete the journey was John Ross's wife, Quatie, who died near Little Rock, Arkansas, of exposure, after giving her blanket to a sick child.

Once the surviving Cherokee arrived in the new territory, they encountered the Old Settlers and Ridgites (those who supported the treaty party and moved before relocation). Both groups had their own ideas about how the new territory should be governed and tensions built quickly and ended in several bloody clashes. In July 1839, both Ridges and Boudinot were killed. Stand Watie was the only one targeted for death to escape the previously mentioned Blood Law killings. For seven years after relocation, the Cherokee Nation continued to fight with the Old Settlers and Ridgites, until a treaty was signed in 1846. Things then remained fairly quiet until the Civil War began.

At the beginning of the Civil War the Cherokees attempted to remain neutral, but that was not to last. This was due in part to the strife and divisions created by the removal of 1838–39, but in addition to the fact that a number of Cherokee were also slave owners. Some sided with the Union (mostly the Old Settlers), and a group—under Stand Watie—pledged allegiance to the Confederacy, as did most of those still living in the east.

Watie was three-quarter Cherokee, and was born December 12, 1806. He learned to speak English at a mission school, and became a planter. Early on, he helped his half-brother Elias Boudinot with the publication of the *Cherokee Phoenix*. Watie raised a company in 1861, was soon appointed colonel of the 1st Cherokee Mounted Rifles, and then later raised to brigadier general. The Cherokee under Watie were engaged in the battles of Wilson's Creek and Elkhorn Tavern, and were principally used in raids and as skirmishers in the Territory and along

its borders. Watie was the last general of the Confederacy to "strike the colors," on June 23, 1865, at Doaksville in Choctaw Nation, more than two months after Gen. Robert E. Lee surrendered.

Today, the Cherokee are considered to be among the most stable and prosperous of all American Indian tribes. All three groups host festivals and events, but the largest of these is the Cherokee National Holiday, held on Labor Day weekend each year and hosted by the Cherokee Nation in Oklahoma. Between 80,000 and 90,000 Cherokee citizens travel to Tahlequah, Oklahoma, for the annual festivities. The Cherokee Nation also still publishes the *Cherokee Phoenix* (both in print and online), a tribal newspaper that has operated continuously since 1828. Editions of the *Cherokee Phoenix* are published in both English and Cherokee Syllabary.

Demography

Among the oldest settlers of North America, the Cherokee inhabited much of the Southeastern United States at the time of the first sustained European contact in the 1600s. Their range included a vast area of about 40,000 square miles (25.6 million acres) covering all of what is now Kentucky, most of Tennessee, and parts of West Virginia, Virginia, North Carolina, South Carolina, Georgia, Alabama, and perhaps a small corner of northern Mississippi. Echota, a settlement on the south bank of the Little Tennessee River, seems to have been considered the early capital of the Cherokee nation.

Of all Eastern tribes, the Cherokee were among the most tolerant and accepting of whites, and they readily adapted to their culture and dress. However, the whites, spurred by land lust and fear of "murdering savages," were not as accepting and wanted Indians off "their" land. Thomas Jefferson played a large role in their removal, beginning with the Louisiana Purchase of 1803. He felt that the federal government should move all eastern tribes westward.

By about 1830, when the Indian Removal Act was signed, and a few years before the forced removal of 1838–39, the Cherokee Nation had been reduced to a population of approximately 20,000 (the reduction being mostly through smallpox epidemics) and lived in an area including only small parts of North Carolina, Georgia, and Alabama—less than a quarter of what they had held only a century earlier. The present-day Cherokee reservation in North Carolina is about 56,688 acres, and their Oklahoma reservations include about 877,000 more acres, for a combined total of about 3½ percent of the lands they owned originally.

By the late 1700s, a conservative band of Cherokee, who wished to maintain a more traditional lifestyle, began moving to what is now Arkansas. This group, known as the Old Settlers, continued to relocate until 1828, when they signed a new treaty with the United States to move further west to a seven million acre tract in Oklahoma. Those families who moved between 1817 and 1835 were given a rifle, kettle, five pounds of tobacco, and a blanket for each person. This group, also known as the Western Cherokee, is now the Keetoowah Band.

For those Cherokee who remained in the east, more hard times were coming. Despite having faced the same hardships as most other Indian tribes, including decimation by smallpox and other diseases, warfare, and lean times as the natural resources were consumed by whites, the Cherokee had another major blow dealt to them—the forced removal from their native lands, along routes which are now usually known as the Trail of Tears. That move, during the winter of 1838–39, cost the tribe nearly a quarter (more than 4,000) of its remaining number, as death on the trail was common.

Yet, according to the 2000 U.S. Census, the Cherokee are now the most numerous of the 563 federally recognized Native American tribes in the United States, with more than 300,000 registered

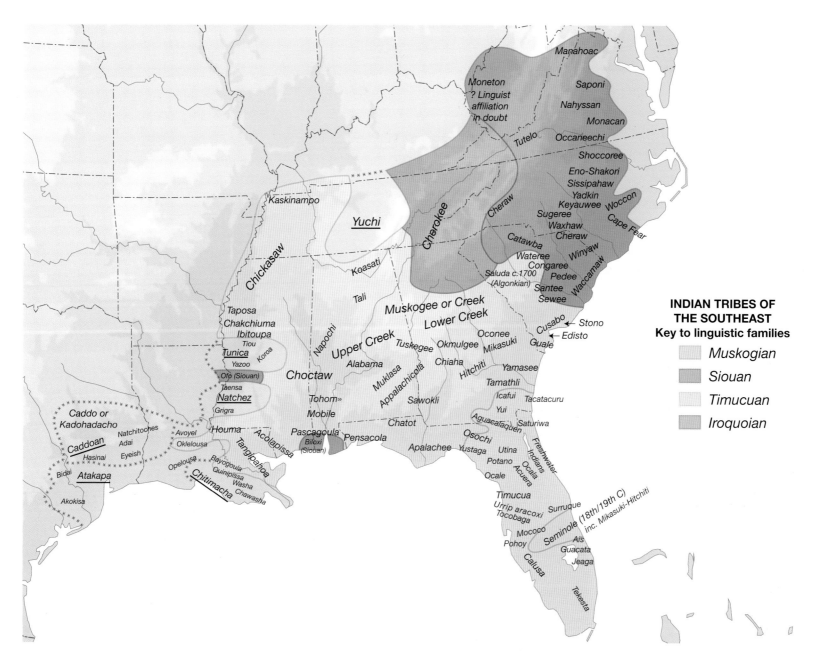

Manahoac

Moneton
? Linguist
affiliation
in doubt

Saponi

Nahyssan

Monacan

Tutelo

Occaneechi

Shoccoree

Eno-Shakori
Sissipahaw
Yadkin
Keyauwee
Sugeree
Waxhaw
Cheraw
Catawba
Wateree
Congaree
Saluda c.1700
(Algonkian)
Santee
Sewee

Woccon

Cape Fear

Winyaw

Waccamaw

Pedee

Kaskinampo

Yuchi

Cherokee

Cheraw

Koasati

Tali

Muskogee or Creek
Lower Creek

Cusabo ← Stono
← Edisto
Guale

Chickasaw

Napochi

Upper Creek

Tuskegee

Okmulgee
Oconee
Mikasuki

Taposa
Chakchiuma
Ibitoupa
Tiou
Tunica
Yazoo
Koroa
Ofo (Siouan)
Taensa
Natchez
Grigra

Alabama

Muklasa
Appalachicola

Chiaha

Hitchiti

Chiaha

Yamasee

Tamathli

Choctaw

Sawokli

Icafui
Yui

Tacatacuru

Caddo or
Kadohadacho
Natchitoches
Adai
Caddoan
Hasinai
Eyeish
Bidai
Atakapa
Akokisa

Avoyel
Oklelousa
Opelousa

Houma

Tohom»

Mobile

Chatot

Pascagoula
Biloxi
(Siouan)

Pensacola

Apalachee

Osochi
Yustaga

Saturiwa

Aguaealaquen

Freshwater
Indians
Utina
Potano
Acuera
Ocale

Acolapissa

Tangipahoa

Bayogoula
Quinipissa
Washa
Chawasha
Chitimacha

Timucua
Urrip aracoxi
Tocobaga

Surruque

Mococo

Pohoy

Calusa

Ais
Guacata
Jeaga

Seminole (18th/19th C)
inc. Mikasuki-Hitchiti

Tekesta

**INDIAN TRIBES OF
THE SOUTHEAST**
Key to linguistic families

Muskogian

Siouan

Timucuan

Iroquoian

members—more than ten times the number alive at the time of the Trail of Tears—but only about one-third actually live on a reservation. Cherokee Indians can be found in every state and in many foreign countries. Of the total number of registered Cherokee, only about 15,000 are identified as full-blood. Most are mixed-blood from extensive intermarriage over the years to both blacks and whites.

There are three federally recognized Cherokee groups with the Bureau of Indian Affairs, given in 2001 as :

1. *Oklahoma Cherokee (Cherokee Nation)*
   Enrollment only requires proof of Western Cherokee ancestry.   228, 307

2. *United Keetoowah Band*
   A sub-group of 1. These are descendants of members of a 19th century society in the

Tribes of the Southeastern Woodlands, c. 1600–1730. The boundaries are, of course, approximate. Modern state boundaries shown with broken lines. Underlined names indicate small linguistic groupings distinct from the larger ones indicated by the shading key. *From Encyclopedia of Native Tribes of North America*

RIGHT: Ancient remains from Etowah Mound. Some 350 burials from the Etowah Mound village have been studied. The data provided a wealth of information regarding burial practices, dress, diet, diseases, trade patterns, and ceremonial practices. *Museum of the Cherokee Indian*

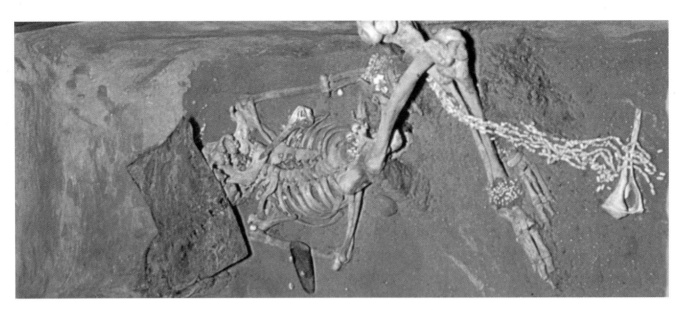

BELOW: Etowah Indian Mounds State Historic Site. *Raymond Gehman/Corbis*

southeast part of the old Cherokee Nation in Oklahoma who have reported themselves separately in the most recent census.   7,953

3. Eastern Cherokee of the Qualla Reservation, North Carolina who require $\frac{1}{32}$ Cherokee ancestry for enrollment.   12,139

It is estimated that 40–50 percent of these Cherokee live within the borders of the old Cherokee Nation or on the Qualla Reservation.

ABOVE: The Etowah Mound settlement (1000–1500 CE) in northeastern Georgia is one of the largest of all mound-builder sites. Etowah inhabitants are thought by many to be early Cherokee. Based on artifacts found, Etowah inhabitants had contact with numerous tribes. *Museum of the Cherokee Indian*

LEFT: Bill Junaluska, a descendant of the man thought to have saved Andrew Jackson's life, stands in his driveway, c. 1950s. Lodging signs appealing to tourists can be seen in the background. *Museum of the Cherokee Indian*

This map of Alabama, from 1826, shows settlements, county boundaries, roads, and topographical features. Also depicted are reservations for the Upper Creek Indians, Cherokee Indians, and Choctaw Indians. Two years later the Indian land was gone.
Michael Maslan Historic Photographs/Corbis

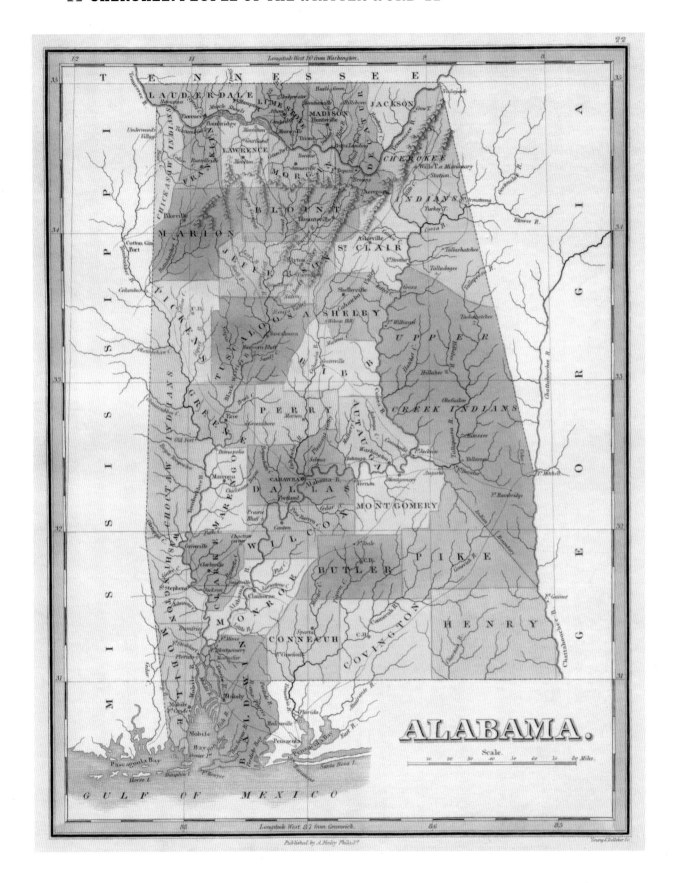

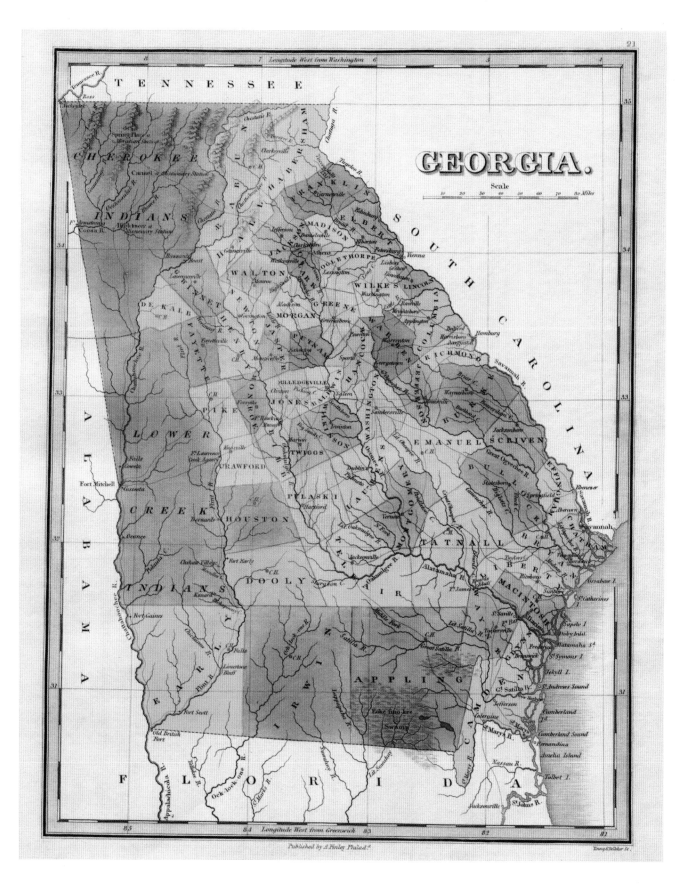

A pre-removal map of Georgia (1826) shows, among other features, a large reservation for the Cherokee that covered much of the northern end of the state. By the time this map was made, Georgia was already preparing to open the land to settlers. *Michael Maslan Historic Photographs/Corbis*

An unidentified Cherokee home in the hills near Cherokee, North Carolina, shows both the natural beauty of the area and the numerous hiding places for those who resisted forced removal. *Museum of the Cherokee Indian*

By the 1950s, when this photo was taken of the Jarrett Blythe home (with Blythe and his wife in the foreground), the Eastern Band Cherokee were living like most other Americans, although not as affluent. *Museum of the Cherokee Indian*

ABOVE: The Qualla Boundary Cherokee Reservation lies adjacent to the Great Smoky Mountains in some of the most picturesque country in North Carolina. The area lies in the heart of ancestral Cherokee grounds. *Museum of the Cherokee Indian*

LEFT: A shallow but broad stream features the beauty of both a mirror-like surface and the texture created by rocks. The misty hills near the Great Smoky Mountains can be seen in the background. *Museum of the Cherokee Indian*

RIGHT: "Indian Territory." After the Trail of Tears, this is where the tribes of the southwest were boundaried in around 1891. *From Encyclopedia of Native Tribes of North America*

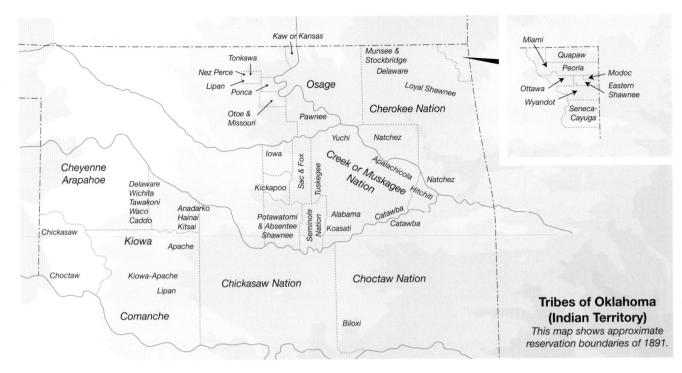

Tribes of Oklahoma (Indian Territory)
This map shows approximate reservation boundaries of 1891.

OPPOSITE: The Oconaluftee Indian Village was established to re-create a model of a working Cherokee village of the past. An unidentified group from the 1970s is shown working on different crafts. *Museum of the Cherokee Indian*

Today's Cherokee

There are over 50 organizations in at least 12 states who lay claim to Cherokee descent, some of whom were reported in the self-identifying 2000 census as follows:

Cherokee   281,069
    (Mainly Western Cherokee of Oklahoma)
Eastern Cherokee   8,166
    (Reservation and parcels N Carolina)
Western Cherokee   5,744
Echota Cherokee   4,066
    (Alabama and Georgia)
Northern Cherokee Nation of Missouri and Arkansas   1,605
    Benton Washington, Sebastian Counties, Arkansas; and Jasper and Newton Counties, Missouri
Cherokee (NE Alabama)   674
Cherokee (SE Alabama)   612

Four Winds Cherokee   605
United Keetoowah Band of Cherokee   528
    (A conservative sub-group of Oklahoma Cherokee in the southern part of the old Cherokee Nation who now require ¼ Cherokee ancestry for membership)
White River Band of the Chickamauga Cherokee   223
Georgia Eastern Cherokee   192
Southeastern Cherokee Council   178
Cherokee (Alabama)   93
Cherokee of Georgia   62

A group in Pennsylvania (Keating Mountain), the "Atlamaha" in Georgia, and the Lumbee of North Carolina have all been attributed some Cherokee ancestry either by themselves or some historians, at some point.

OPPOSITE: Cherokee Territory since White Contact. This map shows how rapidly the vast domain of the Cherokee shrank from the 16th to the 19th centuries. The heart of the ancestral Cherokee Nation is not far from the current Eastern Band Reservation in Cherokee, North Carolina.

History

According to Cherokee legend, in the beginning there was no land—only sea—and all animals lived in a rock vault in the sky. Water Beetle decided to explore the sea and dove to the bottom, bringing back soft mud that spread and became the island of Earth. The flapping of the vulture's wings created the mountains, and the animals ordered the sun to move from the east to the west. Then *Kanati* (First Man) and *Selu* (First Woman) were created. (*Selu* is also the word for corn.)

Working from artifacts and remains, archeologists figure the Cherokee have lived in the southeastern United States for about 10,000 years. Among other evidence, ancient pottery shards found were of much the same patterns as Cherokee women were creating near the end of the 19th century. The ancient Kituwah Mound on the Tuckasegee River, near present-day Bryson City, N.C., is considered by many to be the original Cherokee city.

In 1540, a group of gold-seeking Spaniards, led by Hernando de Soto (see pages 36–37), met the Cherokee and wrote of the "red men."

After Europeans began to settle along the eastern seaboard, they began to encounter the Cherokee. An early intentional encounter was the 1673 expedition of James Needham and Gabriel Arthur in the Overhill Cherokee country. The two Virginians did contact the Cherokee, but Needham was killed on the return journey. By the late 1600s, traders were making regular journeys to Cherokee lands, but few left evidence.

By the early 1700s the Cherokee were highly successful and powerful traders, with their main trading partners in Virginia and South Carolina. Although there was trading, the Cherokee remained relatively unaffected by the presence of European colonies until the Tuscarora War. In 1711 the Tuscarora Indians began attacking North Carolina colonists after diplomatic attempts to address various grievances failed, and armies were sent against them. Although the armies were heavily populated by Indians, the Cherokee did not get involved until late in 1712.

The war helped to bind the Indians of the entire southeastern region together, enhancing Indian networks of communication and trade. It also marked the beginning of a British–Cherokee relationship that remained strong for much of the 18th century.

In 1715, just as the Tuscarora War was winding down, the Yamasee War broke out. Indian tribes, including some Cherokee, launched attacks on South Carolina settlements. Both South Carolina and the Lower Creek tried to gain Cherokee support. The Cherokee were split until January 1716, when a delegation of Creek leaders was murdered at the Cherokee town of Tugaloo.

During the early 18th century the Cherokee nation was unified under the "Emperor" Moytoy, with the aid of an unofficial British envoy, Sir Alexander Cuming. In 1730, seven prominent Cherokee traveled with Cuming to England. The

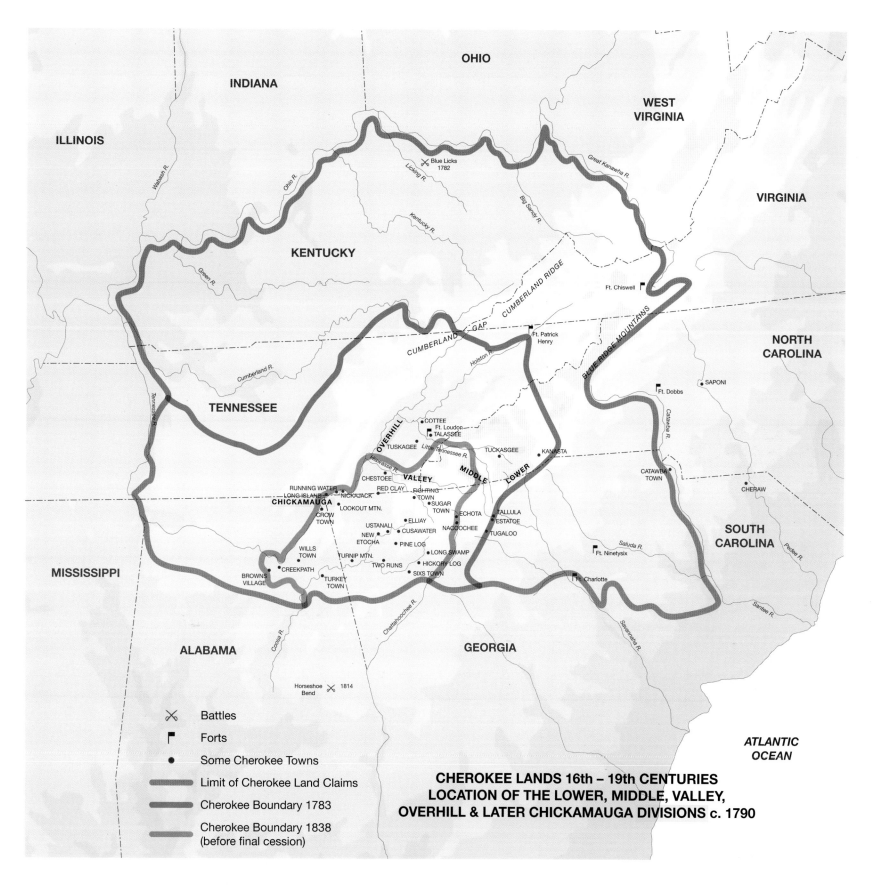

**CHEROKEE LANDS 16th – 19th CENTURIES
LOCATION OF THE LOWER, MIDDLE, VALLEY,
OVERHILL & LATER CHICKAMAUGA DIVISIONS c. 1790**

✕ Battles

⚑ Forts

● Some Cherokee Towns

━━ Limit of Cherokee Land Claims

━━ Cherokee Boundary 1783

━━ Cherokee Boundary 1838
(before final cession)

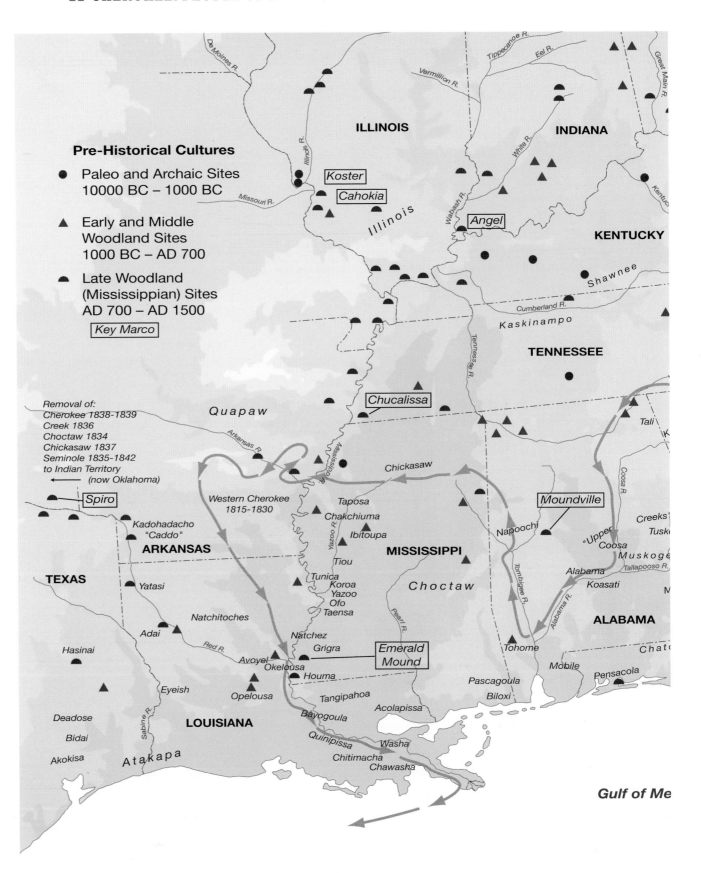

Prehistoric cultural sites and historic native tribes of the southeast. This map shows the principal prehistoric archaeological sites of the southeast and Ohio-Mississippi valleys—note Etowah on page 37 at left center. Note also the route of explorer Hernando de Soto. He died on May 21, 1542, and his expedition returned to Mexico City. Only 300 of the original 700 men survived. *From Encyclopedia of Native Tribes of North America.*

Pre-Historical Cultures

● Paleo and Archaic Sites
10000 BC – 1000 BC

▲ Early and Middle Woodland Sites
1000 BC – AD 700

◗ Late Woodland (Mississippian) Sites
AD 700 – AD 1500

Key Marco

Koster
Cahokia
Angel
Chucalissa
Spiro
Moundville
Emerald Mound

Removal of:
Cherokee 1838-1839
Creek 1836
Choctaw 1834
Chickasaw 1837
Seminole 1835-1842
to Indian Territory
(now Oklahoma)

Western Cherokee
1815-1830

ILLINOIS
INDIANA
KENTUCKY
TENNESSEE
ARKANSAS
TEXAS
MISSISSIPPI
ALABAMA
LOUISIANA

Quapaw
Kadohadacho "Caddo"
Yatasi
Natchitoches
Adai
Hasinai
Deadose
Bidai
Akokisa
Atakapa
Eyeish
Opelousa
Avoyel
Okelousa
Natchez
Grigra
Houma
Bayogoula
Quinipissa
Washa
Chitimacha
Chawasha
Tangipahoa
Acolapissa
Biloxi
Pascagoula
Mobile
Pensacola
Tohome
Koasati
Alabama
Muskoge
Coosa
"Upper
Tuske
Creeks
Tali
Napoochi
Chickasaw
Taposa
Chakchiuma
Ibitoupa
Tiou
Tunica
Koroa
Yazoo
Ofo
Taensa
Choctaw

Shawnee
Kaskinampo

Gulf of Me

De Moines R.
Tippecanoe R.
Eel R.
Vermillion R.
Great Main R.
Illinois R.
Missouri R.
Illinois
Wabash R.
White R.
Kentuc
Cumberland R.
Tennessee R.
Arkansas R.
Mississippi
Yazoo R.
Pearl R.
Tombigbee R.
Alabama R.
Coosa R.
Tallapoosa R.
Red R.
Sabine R.
Chato

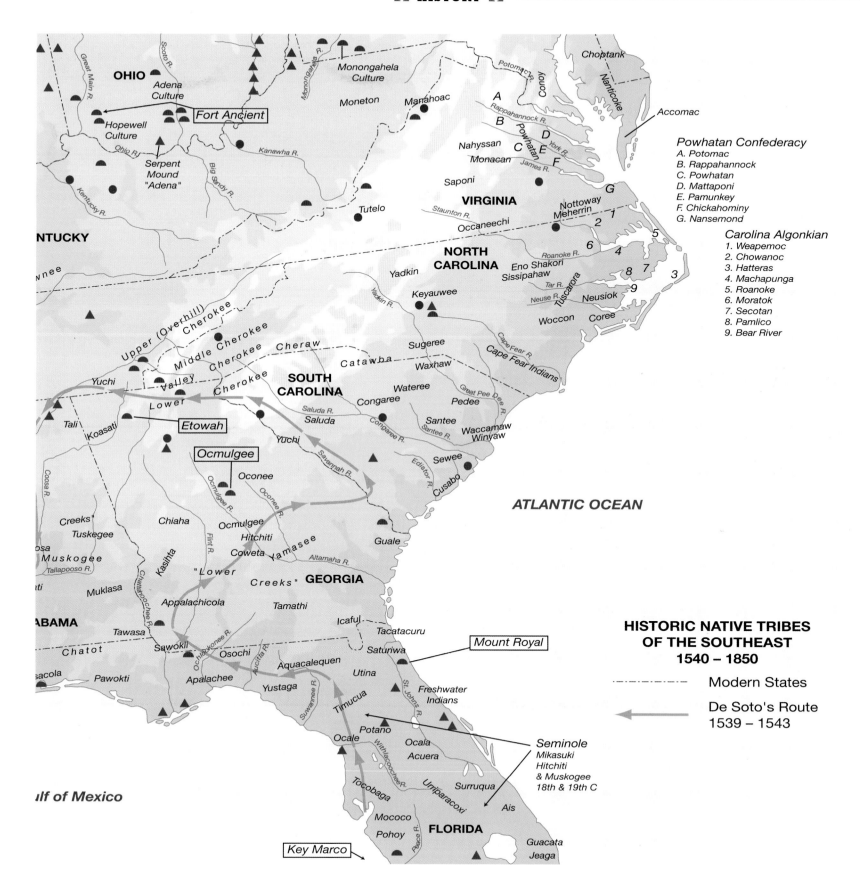

OHIO

Great Main R.

Scioto R.

Adena Culture

Hopewell Culture

Fort Ancient

Monongahela R.

Monongahela Culture

Moneton

Manahoac

Potomac R.

Choptank

Nanticoke

Conoy

Accomac

A

B

C

Nahyssan

Monacan

D

E

F

Powhatan

York R.

James R.

Powhatan Confederacy
A. Potomac
B. Rappahannock
C. Powhatan
D. Mattaponi
E. Pamunkey
F. Chickahominy
G. Nansemond

Serpent Mound "Adena"

Ohio R.

Big Sandy R.

Kanawha R.

Saponi

VIRGINIA

G

Nottoway Meherrin

1

2

5

6

4

7

8

3

9

Carolina Algonkian
1. Weapemoc
2. Chowanoc
3. Hatteras
4. Machapunga
5. Roanoke
6. Moratok
7. Secotan
8. Pamlico
9. Bear River

Kentucky R.

KENTUCKY

Rappahannock R.

Staunton R.

Occaneechi

Tutelo

Roanoke R.

NORTH CAROLINA

Eno Shakori Sissipahaw

Yadkin

Tar R.

Tuscarora

Neusiok

awnee

Yadkin R.

Keyauwee

Neuse R.

Woccon

Coree

Upper (Overhill) Cherokee

Middle Cherokee

Cheraw

Sugeree

Cape Fear R.

Cape Fear Indians

Catawba

Waxhaw

Valley Cherokee

Yuchi

Lower Cherokee

SOUTH CAROLINA

Wateree

Congaree

Pedee

Great Pee Dee R.

Tali

Koasati

Etowah

Saluda R.

Saluda

Congaree R.

Santee

Waccamaw Winyaw

Santee R.

Yuchi

Ocmulgee

Oconee

Savannah R.

Sewee

Edisto R.

Cusabo

ATLANTIC OCEAN

Ocmulgee R.

Chiaha

Ocmulgee

Oconee R.

Hitchiti

Coweta

Yamasee

Guale

Creeks

Tuskegee

Flint R.

Kasihta

Altamaha R.

osa

Muskogee

"Lower Creeks"

GEORGIA

Tallapoosa R.

Muklasa

Appalachicola

Tamathi

ABAMA

Chattahoochee R.

Chatot

Tawasa

Sawokli

Osochi

Icaful

Tacataċuru

Mount Royal

HISTORIC NATIVE TRIBES OF THE SOUTHEAST 1540 – 1850

sacola

Pawokti

Apalachee

Ochlockonee R.

Aucilla R.

Aquacalequen

Utina

Saturiwa

St. Johns R.

Freshwater Indians

— · — · — Modern States

Yustaga

Suwannee R.

Timucua

Ocale

Potano

Ocale

Acuera

Ocala

De Soto's Route 1539 – 1543

Seminole
Mikasuki
Hitchiti
& Muskogee
18th & 19th C

Withlacoochee R.

Surruqua

Tocobaga

Umpiaracoxi

Ais

Gulf of Mexico

Mococo

Pohoy

Peace R.

FLORIDA

Guacata Jeaga

Key Marco

delegation stayed in London for four months, culminating in a formal treaty of alliance between the British and Cherokee, the 1730 Treaty of Whitehall.

Around the time of the Revolutionary War, tribal divisions over continued tolerance of encroachment by white settlers caused some Cherokee to leave the Cherokee Nation. Many of these dissidents became known as the Chickamauga. Led by Chief Dragging Canoe, the Chickamauga made alliances with the Shawnee and engaged in raids against the whites, now known as the Chickamauga Wars.

Some of these early dissidents eventually moved west, across the Mississippi River, to areas that would later become the states of Arkansas and Missouri. Their settlements were established on the St. Francis River and the White River by 1800. Eventually, there were such large numbers of Cherokees in these areas that the U.S. Government in 1815 established a Cherokee Reservation in Arkansas. Cherokee leaders who lived in Arkansas included The Bowl, Sequoyah, Spring Frog and The Dutch. Another band of Cherokee lived in southeast Missouri, western Kentucky and Tennessee in frontier settlements and in European-majority communities around the Mississippi River. These groups later became what is now the Keetoowah Band.

Most of the Cherokee Nation was forcibly relocated west, during the winter of 1838–39 along the Trail of Tears. Not all remaining eastern Cherokees were forced on the Trail of Tears, however. William Holland Thomas, a white store owner, helped more than 600 Cherokee from Qualla Town obtain North Carolina citizenship, making them exempt from removal. More than 400 other Cherokee hid in the remote Snowbird Mountains.

Together, these groups were the basis for what is now the Eastern Band of Cherokees. Out of gratitude to Thomas, they served the Confederacy in the Civil War as part of Thomas' Legion. The legion was the last Confederate unit in the east to surrender. They agreed to cease hostilities on the condition of being allowed to retain their arms for hunting. On the western front Stand Watie's surrender of forces on July 23, 1865, gave the Cherokees the distinction of being the last Confederates to surrender in both theaters of the Civil War.

The Dawes Act of 1887 was a major step in breaking up the tribal basis of Indian lands and government. By the Curtis Act of 1898, this process was extended to include the Oklahoma Cherokee. The Cherokee were forced to dissolve their tribal government and courts on the reservation. Land ownership was no longer to be collective but instead was to be passed on to individuals, many of whom were soon cheated out of their land by white settlers. On March 3, 1906, the Cherokee Nation was officially dissolved, and was not reformed until 1948.

Storming of the Fortress of Neoheroka. Gouache on paper, Ron Embleton, 1930–88. In 1711 Cherokee were given guns by settlers to help drive the Tuscarora Indians (traditional Cherokee enemies) north. The Cherokee later found out that settlers had been supplying guns to other tribes too. It is estimated 900 Indians died in the 1713 Neoheroka battle. *Private Collection/ © Look and Learn/ The Bridgeman Art Library*

LEFT AND BELOW: Cherokee men, probably the mixed bloods Moses Price and Richard Justice, painted by William Hodges in London in 1790–91, when they accompanied William Augustus Bowles during an "unofficial" delegation of Creeks and Cherokee to England in an attempt to re-establish commercial and military activity between the British and the Southern tribes, following the Revolution. *Courtesy of the Royal College of Surgeons, London, UK.*

To the Senate and House of Representatives of the United States of America in Congress assembled:

The Memorial of the undersigned, inhabitants of the City of New-York, respectfully represents,—

THAT in 1791, and shortly after the organization of the Federal Government, a Treaty was concluded between the United States and the Cherokee nation, by which the United States, in the 7th Article of that Treaty, agreed to "solemnly guaranty to the Cherokee nation, all their lands not thereby ceded to the United States:" That by the 6th Article of a Treaty made between the same parties, at Tellico, in 1798, the United States agreed "to continue the guaranty of the remainder of their country for ever:" That these Treaties were solemnly sanctioned by the Senate of the United States, and by George Washington and John Adams; and that their stipulations have not been altered by consent, nor impaired by the conduct, of the Cherokee tribes: That laws were duly passed by Congress to carry into effect those stipulations, by one of which, dated March 30th, 1802, and approved by Thomas Jefferson, all persons are prohibited from making any intrusion upon, or surveying the Indian lands secured by treaty, under a penalty of $1000, and three months imprisonment; and the President of the United States is empowered to enforce the observance of the provisions of that act. Your Memorialists further represent, that the stipulations of those treaties have been faithfully observed, and the provisions of the act of 1802 have been strictly enforced, up to the year 1829; but that since that time, persons acting by virtue of certain pretensions of the State of Georgia, (first advanced within a few years,) have intruded upon the territory thus guarantied to the Cherokee nation, dragged individuals belonging to that tribe to prison, and in various ways have violated their rights, in defiance of the laws and treaties of the United States. Your Memorialists further show, that in equal disregard of the obligations of the Union and the rights of the Indians, by laws recently passed by the Legislature of that State, the Cherokee territory has been formally annexed to the adjacent counties, and provision has been made to survey their lands, and divide them among the citizens of that State, by means of a land lottery.

Your Memorialists further show, that two American citizens, who have settled in the Cherokee country with the sanction of the Federal Government, and with the view of promoting its former humane policy of civilizing the aborigines, have been arrested while peaceably residing within that territory, and condemned to an infamous punishment, which they are now undergoing in a Georgia prison, for no other offence than a refusal to take an oath of allegiance to that State, as a separate member of the confederacy.

Your Memorialists further represent, that no steps have been taken by the Government of the United States, to prevent these manifest violations of its laws and its treaties, or to comply with its solemn guaranty: they would, therefore, as citizens of the United States, and deeply interested in the character of their common country for humanity and good faith, respectfully, but earnestly, entreat your honourable bodies to adopt such measures in the case referred to, as shall enforce the observance of the laws of the Union, preserve inviolate the faith of treaties solemnly executed, vindicate the constitutional authority of the Federal Government, and secure our national character from lasting shame and reproach.

Circular of the New-York Committee in aid of the Cherokee Nation.

SIR,—We address you, and through you the friends of justice and humanity in that part of the country where you reside. We are deeply impressed with the conviction, that great wrongs have been committed against the Cherokee nation, and that still greater are threatened. The faith of the United States has been solemnly plighted to these defenceless persons, in many treaties, which have been ratified by all the forms of the Constitution, President Washington and his four immediate successors uniting with the Senate in the ratification. The other House of Congress has sanctioned these treaties, by passing laws to carry their provisions into effect, and their validity has been recognised in various ways, by every department of the National Government, and also of the State of Georgia.

In utter disregard of these facts, and in violation of these solemn sanctions, the Legislature of Georgia has, within the last four years, passed laws whose direct and only object was the acquisition of the Cherokee lands. In the pursuit of this object, while the public rights of the Cherokee nation have been trampled on, the feelings, the persons, and the property of individuals, have been cruelly outraged.

The Cherokees are desirous and determined to appeal to all competent tribunals for the redress of these wrongs: to the Supreme Court of the United States, as cases shall arise proper for its cognizance: to Congress, by memorials from themselves and their friends, urging the execution of laws and treaties: and finally, to public opinion, presenting to this highest of human tribunals, the unvarnished story of Indian rights and Indian sufferings.

We transmit a copy of the memorial to be sent from this city, and respectfully ask you to co-operate with us in our efforts to aid the Cherokees in the accomplishment of these objects. We would particularly suggest to you the expediency of calling meetings on the subject. Even where two or three only are gathered together in the name of justice, a blessing will attend their deeds. Let such meetings petition Congress—let them make contributions to enable this injured people to defray the expenses of their delegation at Washington—of defending their rights, and of supporting the newspaper (the Cherokee Phœnix) which tells the tale of the outrages they are daily suffering. Above all, let the friends of justice, and the lovers of the real honour of our country, do all in their power, individually and collectively, to diffuse correct information and worthy sentiments on this important subject. Let the virtuous and the high-minded speak out their feelings; let them lend the aid of their zeal and their influence in this holy cause. With such aid, we shall indulge the confident hope, that the right will ultimately and gloriously triumph.

New-York, February 10, 1832.

ELEAZAR LORD,
JOSEPH BLUNT,
M. C. PATERSON,
WM. EMERSON,
} *On behalf of a Committee, appointed at a Public Meeting held in this city, Feb. 1832.*

N. B. Pecuniary contributions may be transmitted to ELEAZAR LORD, Treasurer, at No. 26 Wall-street, New-York, or to either of the above named Committee, and will be devoted to the objects mentioned, according to the best discretion of the Committee.

LEFT AND BELOW LEFT: A circular of the New York Committee in aid of the Cherokee nation was mailed to a number of individuals in February 1832, in an attempt to fight some of the injustices done to the Cherokee in Georgia. *Library of Congress*

ABOVE: Capitol fashions for 1837. A President Martin Van Buren caricature drawn during the Panic of 1837 is critical of his continuation of Andrew Jackson's policies. Van Buren, in a princely cloak, is treading on the Constitution and a paper titled "Indian Claims." *Library of Congress Prints and Photographs Division LC-USZ62-26455*

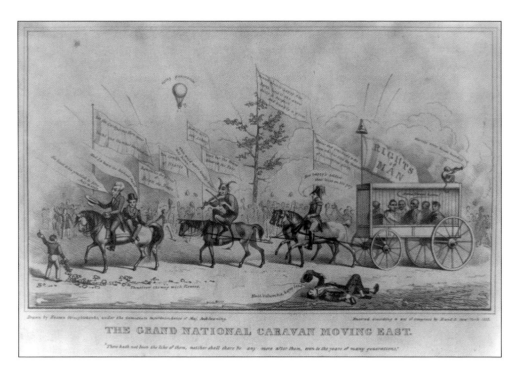

THE GRAND NATIONAL CARAVAN MOVING EAST.

LEFT: A burlesque parade, 1833. President Andrew Jackson is depicted leading a parade satirizing his administration, including his Indian removal policy. At the rear of the parade is a caged wagon, containing Cherokee and other Indians, with a flag "Rights of Man" and liberty cap. One forlorn Indian sings "Home! Sweet home!" *Library of Congress Prints and Photographs Division LC-USZ62-9646*

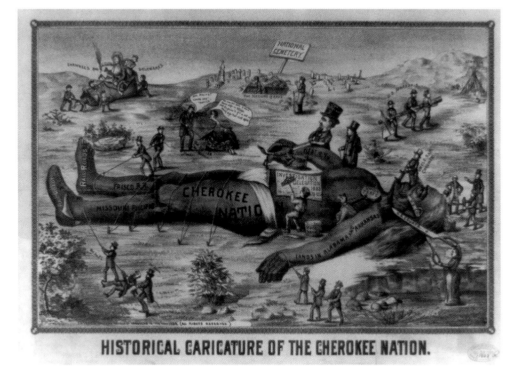

HISTORICAL CARICATURE OF THE CHEROKEE NATION.

ABOVE: Even well after relocation, the Cherokee still had many problems. This 1886 caricature shows the Cherokee Nation as a Gulliver, tied by the many Lilliputians of White policy, including railroads, investigations and attempts at further land grabs. *Library of Congress Prints and Photographs Division LC-USZ62-89733*

RIGHT: Principal Cherokee Towns c. 1720. By the time of forced removal, there were still Cherokee villages dotted across the present states of North Carolina, South Carolina, Georgia, and Tennessee. The current Eastern Band reservation is also shown.

CHEROKEE TOWNS 1755:
Overhill Towns: Great Tellico, Chatuga, Chota, Toqua, Sittiquo (Settilo), Talassee
Valley Towns: Euforsee, Conastee, Little Telliqud (Little Tellico), Cotocanahut, Nayowee, Tomatly, Chewohe (Cheeowee)
Middle Towns: Joree, Watoge, Nuckasee
Keowee Towns: Keowee, Tricentee, Echoee, Torsee, Cowee, Estatoie (Estatoe), Tosawa, Keowee, Oustanelle

CHEROKEE TOWNS 1799:
Oostinawley; Creek Path; Aumoia; Nicojack (Nickajack); Running Water; Ellijay (Elijay); Cabben; High Tower; Pine Log; High Tower Forks; Tocoah; Coosawaytee; Crowtown; Shoemeck; Aumuchee; Tulloolah; Willstown; Acohee; Cuclon; Ducktown; Ailigvlsha; Highwassee (Hiwassee); Lookout Mountain; Noyohee; Tusquittee; Coosa; Nantiyallee; Saukee; Keyukee; Red Bank; Nukeza; Cowpens; Telasse (Talassee); Buffalo Town; Little Tellico; Rabbit Trap; Notley; Turnip Mountain; Sallicoah; Kautika; Tausitu; Watoga (Watauga); Cowee; Chillhoway; Chestuee; Turkey Town; Toquah; Chota; Big Tellico (Great Tellico); Tusskegee (Tuskagee)

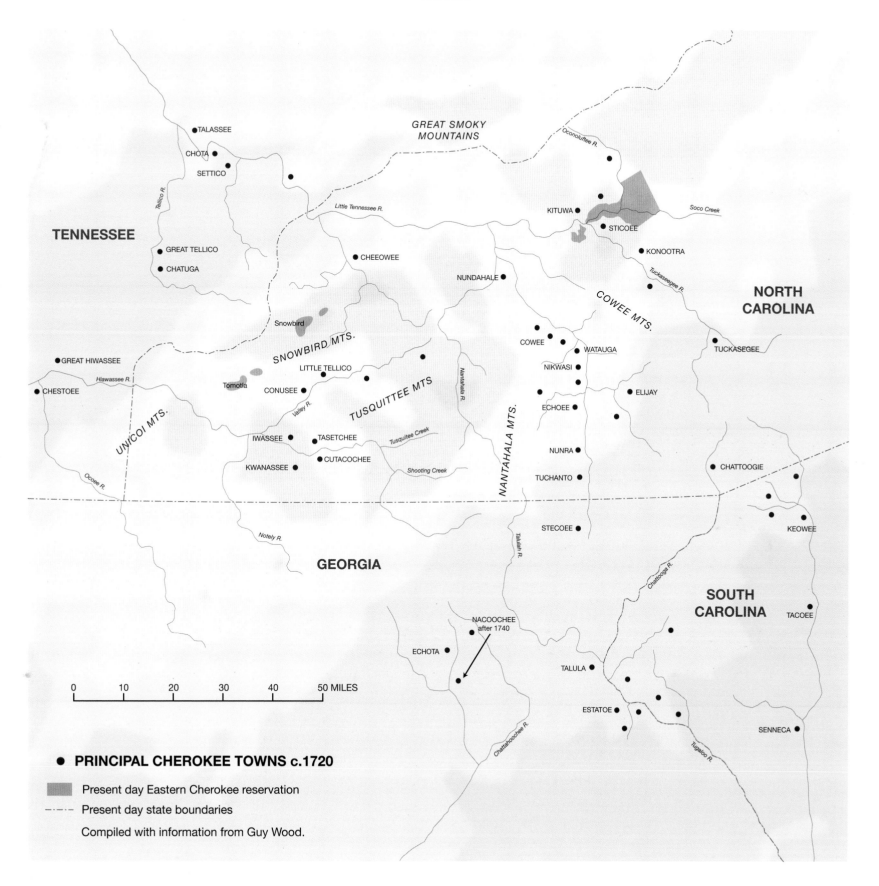

GREAT SMOKY
MOUNTAINS

Oconoluftee R.

Soco Creek

● TALASSEE

CHOTA ●

SETTICO ●

Tellico R.

Little Tennessee R.

KITUWA ●

STICOEE ●

KONOOTRA ●

Tuckaseegee R.

TENNESSEE

GREAT TELLICO ●

CHATUGA ●

● CHEEOWEE

NUNDAHALE ●

COWEE MTS.

**NORTH
CAROLINA**

Snowbird

SNOWBIRD MTS.

COWEE ●

WATAUGA

● TUCKASEGEE

GREAT HIWASSEE ●

Tomotla

LITTLE TELLICO ●

Nantahala R.

NIKWASI ●

Hiawassee R.

CONUSEE ●

TUSQUITTEE MTS

ELIJAY ●

CHESTOEE ●

Valley R.

ECHOEE ●

UNICOI MTS.

IWASSEE ●

TASETCHEE ●

Tusquitee Creek

NANTAHALA MTS.

NUNRA ●

● CHATTOOGIE

KWANASSEE ●

CUTACOCHEE ●

Shooting Creek

TUCHANTO ●

Ocoee R.

KEOWEE ●

STECOEE ●

Notely R.

Talulah R.

GEORGIA

**SOUTH
CAROLINA**

NACOOCHEE
after 1740

TACOEE ●

0   10   20   30   40   50 MILES

ECHOTA ●

Chattooga R.

TALULA ●

ESTATOE ●

SENNECA ●

Chattahoochee R.

Tugaloo R.

● **PRINCIPAL CHEROKEE TOWNS c.1720**

Present day Eastern Cherokee reservation

Present day state boundaries

Compiled with information from Guy Wood.

RIGHT: This item (lithograph, American school, 19th century) documents the forced removal of the Indians from their homeland in Georgia, from the Georgia point of view. *Private Collection/Peter Newark American Pictures/The Bridgeman Art Library*

FAR RIGHT: Three American Cherokee Chiefs, 1762. American school, 18th century. Although they are dressed in clothing undoubtedly supplied by the British, facial tattoos can clearly be seen on the men in this engraving. Turbans were also frequently provided to visiting Cherokee. *Private Collection/Peter Newark American Pictures/The Bridgeman Art Library*

ACTS

OF THE

STATE OF GEORGIA

AN ACT

To ratify and confirm certain articles of agreement and cession entered into on the 24th day of April 1802, between the Commissioners of the State of Georgia on the one part, and the Commissioners of the United States on the other part.

WHEREAS the Commissioners of the State of Georgia, to wit: James Jackson, Abraham Baldwin, and John Milledge, duly authorized and appointed by, and on the part and behalf of the said State of Georgia; and the Commissioners of the United States, James Madison, Albert Gallatin, and Levi Lincoln, duly authorized and appointed by, and on the part and behalf of the said United States, to make an amicable settlement of limits, between the two Sovereignties, after a due examination of their respective powers, did, on the 24th day of April last, enter into a deed of articles, and mutual cession, in the words following, to wit:

ARTICLES of agreement and cession, entered into on the twenty-fourth day of April, one thousand eight hundred and two, between the Commissioners appointed on the part of the United States, by virtue of an act entitled, "An act for an amicable settlement of limits

Cherokees came over from the head of the River Savanna to London 1762

ABOVE: The Seal of the Cherokee Nation bears the September 6, 1839, date, when the Constitution was adopted, and consists of a seven-point star (representing the seven clans), surrounded by oak (for keeping the sacred fire lit). Lettering from the syllabary appears in the outer ring. *Bettmann/Corbis*

RIGHT: An anti-removal tract (lithograph, American school, 19th century) reproducing part of the arguments heard in *The Cherokee Nation vs. the State of Georgia*. This was published in response to the forced removal of Indians from their homeland, 1831. *Private Collection/Peter Newark American Pictures/The Bridgeman Art Library*

THE CASE

OF

THE CHEROKEE NATION

against

THF STATE OF GEORGIA:

ARGUED AND DETERMINED AT

THE SUPREME COURT OF THE UNITED STATES,

JANUARY TERM 1831.

WITH

AN APPENDIX,

Containing the Opinion of Chancellor Kent on the Case ; the Treaties between the United States and the Cherokee Indians ; the Act of Congress of 1802, entitled ' An Act to regulate intercourse with the Indian tribes, &c.'; and the Laws of Georgia relative to the country occupied by the Cherokee Indians, within the boundary of that State.

BY RICHARD PETERS,
COUNSELLOR AT LAW.

Philadelphia:
JOHN GRIGG, 9 NORTH FOURTH STREET.
1831.

New Echota. The interior of the cabin where the Treaty Party signed the Treaty of New Echota in 1835, leading to the forced removal of the Cherokee. *Museum of the Cherokee Indian*

CHEROKEE IN THE WEST AND THE TRAIL OF TEARS

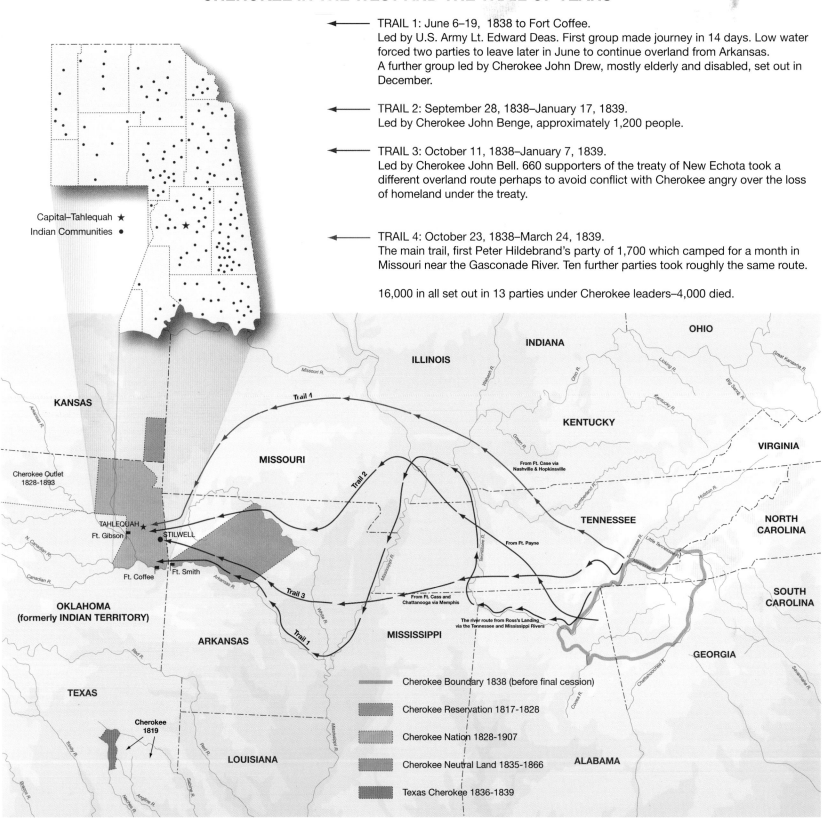

TRAIL 1: June 6–19, 1838 to Fort Coffee.
Led by U.S. Army Lt. Edward Deas. First group made journey in 14 days. Low water forced two parties to leave later in June to continue overland from Arkansas.
A further group led by Cherokee John Drew, mostly elderly and disabled, set out in December.

TRAIL 2: September 28, 1838–January 17, 1839.
Led by Cherokee John Benge, approximately 1,200 people.

TRAIL 3: October 11, 1838–January 7, 1839.
Led by Cherokee John Bell. 660 supporters of the treaty of New Echota took a different overland route perhaps to avoid conflict with Cherokee angry over the loss of homeland under the treaty.

TRAIL 4: October 23, 1838–March 24, 1839.
The main trail, first Peter Hildebrand's party of 1,700 which camped for a month in Missouri near the Gasconade River. Ten further parties took roughly the same route.

16,000 in all set out in 13 parties under Cherokee leaders–4,000 died.

Capital–Tahlequah ★
Indian Communities ●

Cherokee Boundary 1838 (before final cession)
Cherokee Reservation 1817-1828
Cherokee Nation 1828-1907
Cherokee Neutral Land 1835-1866
Texas Cherokee 1836-1839

LEFT: Cherokee in the West and the Trail of Tears. Ten different routes were used by the Indians who were relocated during the Trail of Tears, 1838–39. Variations on the four main routes are shown here. The inset shows Oklahoma Cherokee communities.

ABOVE: Thomas' Legion, Confederate States Army. A group of Civil War veterans of the Eastern Band of the Cherokee pose with a Confederate flag, c. 1890s. The men served with Thomas' Legion in gratitude for his help with establishing the Eastern Reservation. *Museum of the Cherokee Indian*

Cherokee Land Allotment, 1903. This map shows the progress of land allotment to tribal members in the Oklahoma Cherokee Nation in 1903. The Cherokee Nation was officially dissolved in March 1906. *Library of Congress Geography and Map Division ct002107*

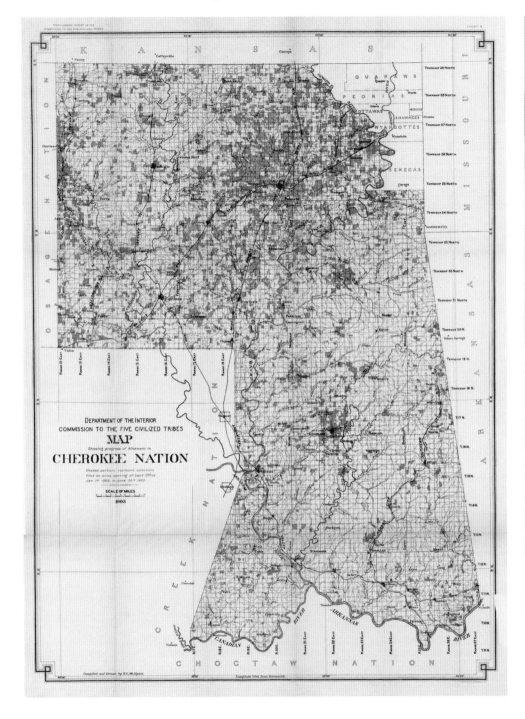

Oklahoma Land Rush of 1893. The taking of Cherokee land did not end with the Trail of Tears. Oklahoma land in what was known as the Cherokee Strip that had belonged to the Cherokee was opened up to settlers in 1893. *Private Collection/Peter Newark Western Americana/The Bridgeman Art Library*

RIGHT: A special ceremony was held in November 1910 for the unveiling of the Junaluska monument. The monument was placed on the grave by the Daughters of the American Revolution, members of which are seen in the background. *Museum of the Cherokee Indian*

RIGHT: Western Cherokee Land, 1864. Prior to having more land taken from them as Civil War reparations, the Cherokee were assigned large tracts of land in Oklahoma. This map shows the territory originally assigned to the Cherokee, as well as boundaries occupied or owned by them in 1864. *Library of Congress Prints and Photographs Division*

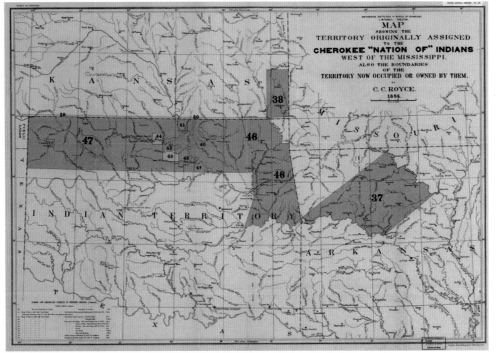

RIGHT: The Junaluska Monument seen in the 1940s. Until recently, the Junaluska Monument consisted of a stone with a plaque. In 1997, Friends of Junaluska constructed a seven-sided monument (representing the seven Cherokee clans) around the grave. *Museum of the Cherokee Indian*

ABOVE: A group of Cherokee Indians (players and spectators) take part in a ceremony prior to the traditional Ball Game, *c.* 1880s. The Ball Game, played with sticks and a ball, is a very rough sport that has some similarities to lacrosse. *Museum of the Cherokee Indian*

RIGHT: Spectators and players alike take part in various ceremonial preliminaries to the Ball Game, *c.* 1887. Dozens of people are shown here, surrounding several players with sticks. *Museum of the Cherokee Indian*

ABOVE: A group of Ball Game players struggles for the ball with their sticks during a game, *c.* 1887. The ball, made from deerskin, is stuffed with deer hair. *Museum of the Cherokee*

LEFT: Many tribal members—spectators and players—bet on the Ball Game. The men shown are holding the bets, which consist of clothing, personal possessions and other items. *c.* 1887 *Museum of the Cherokee Indian Indian*

BELOW: Ball Game player Joe Crow strikes a pose with stick in hand, *c. 1880s.* Sticks have a looped head with net. If a player dropped his stick, he had to carry the ball with his teeth. *Museum of the Cherokee Indian*

BELOW: The Carlisle, Pennsylvania, Indian School, which tried to eliminate all Indian behavior, had ball games, but they were quite different from the traditional Cherokee ones. A Cherokee baseball player at Carlisle is shown here, date unknown. *Museum of the Cherokee Indian*

ABOVE: This group of Cherokee students was photographed a few months after arriving at the Hampton Normal and Agricultural Institute. Often the school took "before and after" photos to show "Civilization progress." *Museum of the Cherokee Indian*

RIGHT: The Hampton Normal and Agricultural Institute worked very hard to "civilize" Indians. This undated photo shows Cherokee students arriving at the school. Because of generations of acculturation, they were more "civilized" than most Indians. *Museum of the Cherokee Indian*

Cultural Traditions

Cherokee culture is loaded with many interesting facets, but one of the most intriguing of these is the historical relationship between men and women in the tribe. Inheritance, including familial association, was matrilineal, and when a couple married, the male went to live with the female's clan.

Domestic work was divided similarly to many cultures, with the man hunting and the woman gathering and gardening—but with a twist. While it was expected that the husband would share all of his hunting bounty with his wife and children, the garden and all gathered produce belonged very specifically to the wife. It was entirely up to her whether she shared any with her husband. If a couple split up, the male simply left the hut, leaving it and all possessions behind.

Polygamy was an acceptable practice, and a brave could have as many wives as he wished, as long as he observed all customary laws of the clan. The practice, and the reasons for it, were things European settlers never fully understood. Because of hard life, warfare and disease, a high birth rate was necessary to keep a clan and the tribe healthy and growing.

Clans were an extremely important aspect of Cherokee life. The Cherokee were divided into seven clans, including the Wild Potato (plant knowledge), Wolf (warriors), Deer (hunters), Bird (messengers), Red Paint (healers), Blue Holly (healers for children) and Long Hair (historians and chiefs). Marriages within clans were never allowed. Since all inheritance was matrilineal, children were considered to have descended from their mother's clan, rather than that of their father. Because the Cherokee believed that all members of a clan descended from a specific ancestor, all clan members were related. Thus, a Deer clan member could expect to receive food, shelter and acceptance from those of the Deer clan wherever he traveled—even if he did not know them. Clan ties were so strong that there was no need for either a form of police or court system. All protection, justice and retribution were meted out by the clan to achieve balance within the tribe. Clans formally relinquished their judicial responsibilities in the 1820s, when the Cherokee Supreme Court was established.

The matrilineal clan definition was broken in 1825, when the National Council extended citizenship to biracial children of Cherokee men. As a result, clan membership no longer defined Cherokee citizenship. The 1827 Constitution stated that "No person who is of negro or mulatlo [sic] parentage, either by the father or mother side, shall be eligible to hold any office of profit, honor or trust under this Government," with the exception of "negroes and descendants of white and Indian men by negro women who may have been set free." This set the stage later for the emergence of the Cherokee Freedmen, tribal members who are descendants of slaves once owned by the Cherokee.

Balance and harmony were exceedingly important to the Cherokee, and religious observance (which merged with daily life) focused on the maintenance of a pure, balanced world. Bathing, gardening, singing and hunting all had religious overtones. Hunters, for example, asked a deer's pardon when killing it.

Another Cherokee belief was essentially "you are what you eat." Thus, stickball players never ate rabbit meat (rabbits are easily confused), and pregnant women would not eat squirrel, lest the baby go up, instead of down, during delivery.

Language-wise, there seem to have been a number of minor dialects spoken within the Cherokee, but their distant linguistic connection is with the Iroquoian, although their separation may have taken place more than 2,000 years ago.

The Cherokee language is unusual, in that it does not contain any "r"-based sounds. As such, the word "Cherokee," when spoken in the language, is expressed as *Tsa-la-gi* (pronounced "jah-la-gee"). There are two main dialects spoken by modern Cherokee. The Giduwa dialect is spoken by the Eastern Band, and the Otali Dialect (also called Overhill) is spoken in Oklahoma.

The Language

The written nature of the Cherokee language has helped it to survive, where many Indian languages have died out in the past two centuries. The language has, however, changed a bit (as does any living language). The Otali dialect includes many contracted and borrowed words that have been added since Sequoyah's time, for example.

Still, there is concern among all three bands that there are not enough speakers of the language to keep it vibrant. One of the programs to combat this trend is "immersion teaching," which essentially forces children to learn the language by having teachers communicate with students in the language.

Wahnenauhi (Mrs Lucy L. Keys), a mixed-blood Western Cherokee lady of distinguished ancestry, connected by blood and marriage to the most prominent families in the Cherokee Nation. She was born at Willstown, Alabama, in 1831, and lived in the west at Park Hill, Oklahoma. Although a Christian and a part of the wealthy, educated mixed-blood class, she presented to the Bureau of American Ethnology a manuscript of Cherokee historical "customs, traditions, and superstitions" which remains an important social document of its time. *From a photograph provided by her grandson Clum D. Keys.*

This type of teaching theory is most effective with younger children, while the learning centers of their brains are still developing. For example, three classrooms at the Tribal Child Care Center in Cherokee, N.C., with children ranging from infants to three-year-olds, hear and speak only Cherokee. The children learn English from their families and the broader environment. This program has been successful enough that there are plans to extend the Cherokee Language Immersion Program through the fifth grade.

This 1940s-era photo shows Osley B. Saunooke and his family posing with his boxing club. As "Chief" Saunooke, he became the world heavyweight wrestling champion when he defeated Tom Johnson in a grudge match staged in Boston in 1938. *Museum of the Cherokee Indian*

There are older students and adults on all three reservations who also wish either to learn or improve their Cherokee language skills. The challenge is finding enough people with the necessary language skills to become certified teachers. To help with this, Western Carolina University is working on developing a Cherokee Language Academy, which will include language courses and certification programs from which students can be recruited to become language teachers.

This 1940s-era photo shows Osley B. Saunooke and his family posing with his boxing club. As "Chief" Saunooke, he became the world heavyweight wrestling champion when he defeated Tom Johnson in a grudge match staged in Boston in 1938. *Museum of the Cherokee Indian*

A traditional way of grinding corn and other grains was to hollow out the end of a log, creating a natural mortar. The pestle is also fashioned of wood. *c.* 1940s. *Museum of the Cherokee Indian*

LEFT: Maude Welch, a well-known Cherokee potter, is shown in this photo as an elderly woman in her home, surrounded by a lifetime of memories. Today, her pots sell for hundreds of dollars. *Museum of the Cherokee Indian*

RIGHT: After the Great Smoky Mountains opened the tourist trade for the Eastern Cherokee in the 1930s, talented crafts-people such as Maude Welch (shown making pottery) enjoyed some commercial success. *Museum of the Cherokee Indian*

A little girl in Western dress holds her doll as she scowls at the camera. The doll, also in Western dress, is a typical porcelain-head type of the time. *c.* 1900. *Museum of the Cherokee Indian*

Making functional and traditional Cherokee crafts was a regular part of day-to-day life for many of the Eastern Band. Johnson Catolster, a bowlmaker, is shown in this 1940s-era photo with his family. *Museum of the Cherokee Indian*

ABOVE: Although much grinding was done by hand, some Cherokee used labor-saving devices such as the corn-pounding-mill shown here in this undated photo. The basic structure is the same as the mortar and pestle. *Museum of the Cherokee Indian*

LEFT: Two elderly women are shown on the stoop of their cabin, making pottery by hand in this undated photo. Note the wooden mortar and pestle in the background. *Museum of the Cherokee Indian*

ABOVE: A woman (possibly part Cherokee) with three Cherokee children poses in European-style clothing in this late-19th-century photo. The little girl in her lap was moving too fast for the shutter. *Museum of the Cherokee Indian*

RIGHT: A 1942 photo shows a portion of Cherokee, North Carolina, on Highway 19, facing Bryson City. Although there are buildings in town, much of the natural landscape is unchanged. *Museum of the Cherokee Indian*

ABOVE: Tommy Smith, a young Cherokee boy in 1884, when this photo was taken, poses standing on a crate in a gown, smiling at the camera. *Museum of the Cherokee Indian*

An unidentified group of elementary school children plays on a school playground, taking turns pushing swings in Cherokee, North Carolina, *c.* 1950s. *Museum of the Cherokee Indian*

Since not long after first contact with whites, Christianity has had deep roots within the Cherokee people. Two young girls are shown decorating a Christmas tree during the 1950s. *Museum of the Cherokee Indian*

RIGHT: In early 1946, when this photo was taken, the Eastern Band was supporting legislation to limit tribal membership to Indians with more than one-sixteenth blood to prevent "White Indians" from making claims on the reservation. This woman was carrying her child in a "traditional" manner. *Bettmann/Corbis*

OPPOSITE: In 1945, the Eastern Band of Cherokee decided to embrace the tourist trade. They opened lodging facilities and set up "trading posts" with various Indian crafts to sell to those driving through Cherokee, North Carolina. A promotional photo shows a boy watching Carl Standingdeer whittle a bow. *Bettmann/Corbis*

Cherokee Alphabet

Sounds represented by vowels.

a as a in father or short as a in rival
e as a in hate or short as e in met
i as i in pique or short as i in pit

o as aw in law or short as o in not
u as oo in fool or short as u in pull
v as u in but, nasalized.

Consonant Sounds.

g nearly as in English, but approaching to k. d nearly as in English, but approaching to t. h, k, l, m, n, q, s, t, w, y, as in English.
Syllables beginning with g, except ꮪ have sometimes the power of k, ꭰ, ꭲ ꮹ are sometimes sounded to, tu, tv; and syllables written with tl,
except ꮡ sometimes vary to dl.

Pendleton's Lithography, Boston.

LEFT: Soon after Sequoyah devised the Cherokee syllabary, most of the tribe became literate. The first Cherokee newspaper, the *Cherokee Phoenix*, was established in 1825. This example is from February 21, 1828. *American Antiquarian Society/Bridgeman Art Library*

OPPOSITE: Cherokee Alphabet, from Pendelton's *Lithography*, 1835. This engraving shows the Cherokee "alphabet" created by Sequoyah. It actually is a syllabary, as each character represents a syllable of speech. *Library of Congress/Bridgeman Art Library*

BELOW: A bilingual notice from the *Cherokee Phoenix* of May 18, 1828, showing the Cherokee language in everyday use. *Library of Congress LC-DIG-ppmsca-02912*

Cherokee

(1820) M. Martin.

RIGHT: A 1909 panoramic shot of a portion of the Qualla Boundary Cherokee Indian Reservation near Cherokee, North Carolina, shows a large pasture, with homes and the ancestral hills of the Cherokee in the background. *Library of Congress Prints and Photographs Division LC-USZ62-71820 and 71821*

RIGHT: Promoting literacy and education have always been important priorities of the Cherokee. Shown is the Cherokee Reading Club of 1949. Note the Indian-related book titles on the bulletin board. *Museum of the Cherokee Indian*

LEFT: A watercolor sketch from 1820 by Anne Marguerite Hyde de Neuville (c. 1749–1849) shows a Cherokee in native dress standing, facing right, carrying rods and a bundle. The clothing worn by this Indian appears to be from an earlier time. *New York Historical Society/Bridgeman Art Library*

ON THE INDIAN RESERVATION   CHEROKEE, N.C.

CHEROKEE INDIAN READING CLUB

Material Culture

Unfortunately for historians, much true traditional Cherokee material culture was lost long before ethnographers ever thought to begin documenting the tribe. The Cherokee were among the first and most successful at adopting the dress, culture, and tools of the Europeans. By the late 1600s the Cherokee were already actively trading furs and skins with the Europeans for metal implements such as pots, pans, knives, axes, and other tools—and guns, which they soon came to depend on. This adaptability helped the Cherokee survive, but it did cost them much of their traditional culture. Nonetheless we do have some information on pre-white-contact Cherokee civilization.

Early Cherokee villages were typically contained in stockades (for protection from both animals and enemies), made up of long, pointed poles set in the ground. Villages were usually located near streams and rivers. At the time the whites came in contact with the Cherokee, they were still (for the most part) living in these stockades—and it has been suggested that the early log cabins and forts of the pioneers were copied from those of the Cherokee.

There were two types of huts used by the Cherokee, one for summer and one for winter habitation. Both were constructed of a sapling or cut-wood frame and covered with grass and clay. In some cases, mats were woven from grasses and hung on the frames before plastering. Summer homes were usually rectangular and were larger than the winter home, or *aji*, which was small and domed to conserve heat. Most homes had a single door, no windows, and a vent hole to allow smoke to escape from the fire inside. Most summer cooking was done outdoors.

For most of their pre-European contact period, the Cherokee relied primarily on hunting game (which was plentiful) and gathering nuts, berries, and other edible vegetation. Hunting weapons consisted of the bow and arrow, tomahawk, flint blades, and the blowgun.

Over time, the Cherokee began to develop more of a gardening culture, cultivating corn, squash, other vegetables, and tobacco, which was first used ceremonially, then for general use. As the Cherokees' cultivation culture grew, so did their use of pottery vessels, which eventually became fairly ornate.

Clothing for men was likely deerskin breechcloth, deerskin shirt, and a feathered cloak, while women wore a short deerskin skirt.

Transportation was either on foot or by dugout canoe, large logs hollowed out through burning and scraping. Horses were not a part of Cherokee culture until relatively late.

Many depictions of the Cherokee (including the best-known image of Sequoyah) show them dressed in turbans and jackets. While these garments became—in fact—traditional, their use originated with European contact. As the British began negotiating with the Cherokee for their fur trade, they occasionally took delegations of Indians back to

England. Because the tattooed heads and bodies of the Indians were considered to be too savage for British royalty, the Indians were given turbans for their heads and smoking jackets, much like the clothing worn by Muslim servants. These clothing styles became popular with the Cherokee and continue to be "traditional" among the tribe.

BELOW: A traditional-style Cherokee summer hut, built from saplings covered with grass and clay, is among the dwellings reconstructed as exhibits of the Cherokee National Museum in Tahlequah, Oklahoma. *Danny Lehman/Corbis*

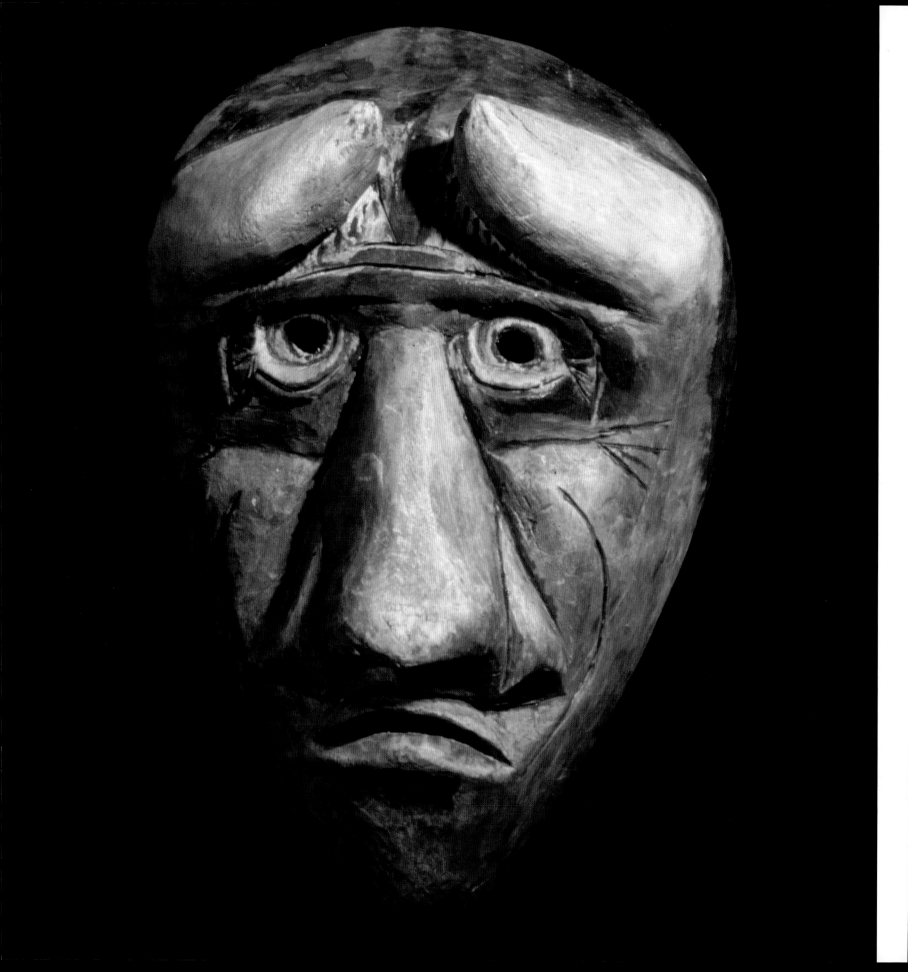

OPPOSITE: Making masks is a very old tradition in Cherokee culture. Although this mask is made of wood, a number of them also are made from large gourds. *Art Archive/Cherokee Indian Museum/Mireille Vautier*

LEFT: A wooden mask that was used for the Cherokee Snake Dance. Although the Cherokee are known primarily for other dances, the Snake Dance is thought to be ancient. *Art Archive/ Cherokee Indian Museum/ Mireille Vautier*

RIGHT AND BELOW RIGHT: "Cherokee" patent medicines. Labels from white-created 1860s' patent medicines. Cherokee Remedy (below) cures "when all other prescriptions fail." The "medicine" likely contained heroin. The image shows an Indian offering herbs to a half-naked squaw. *Library of Congress Prints and Photographs Division LC-USZ62-55634*

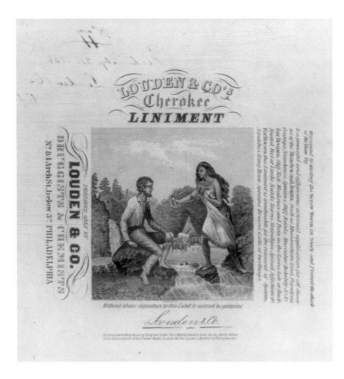

FAR RIGHT: Cherokee chief *c.* 1825. The ceremonial dress of Southeastern leaders at the time of removal to Indian Territory mixed European materials with native styles. Moccasins remained the Eastern center-seam type. Cloth or occasionally buckskin leggings with front seams may have been native derived. This European style coat has an open front and large collar, and the cloth turban features a silver band and imported feathers. Some Cherokee, Creek, and Seminole triangular flap bandolier pouches survive, decorated in antique curving symmetrical beadwork designs of an almost African quality. One example has gold plated beads. *Richard Hook*

ABOVE: Basket with Lid, Cherokee, *c.* 1720. Along with pottery and other crafts, the Cherokee were known for fine basketry. This example of a woven rivercane basket with lid shows a fairly intricate design. *British Museum/Boltin Picture Library/Bridgeman Art Library*

DhGWY

JƏƆOVꓕ JƏꙄGꓕⱭꓕ.

CHEROKEE PRIMER.

-PARK HILL:

Mission Press. John Candy, Printer.

Dꙮ OꚺhBⱭꓵꓭ: ꓮGY�, JꙆBWꙨⱭ.

:::::::

1845.

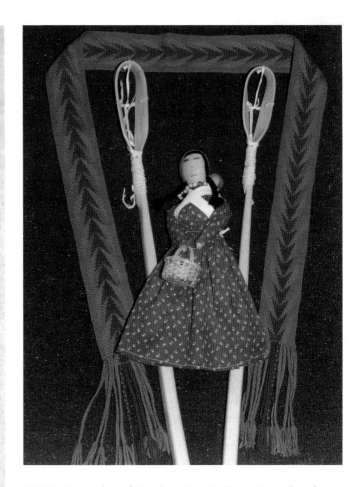

ABOVE: Examples of Southeastern Indian arts and crafts, 20th century. 1. A belt of finger woven wool, made by Mary Shell—Tahlequah, Oklahoma. 2. Doll, woman with baby, Eastern Cherokee, North Carolina, showing the style of dress worn during the 19th century. 3. A pair of ball-game sticks used in two forms of an ancient game still played by descendants of several southeastern tribes.

LEFT: Just as primers were used to teach English to white children, the Cherokee devised primers for their written language. This example from 1845 was used by children in the Cherokee Nation school system. *Private Collection/ Peter Newark American Pictures/Bridgeman Art Library*

ABOVE: Nancy George and her daughter, Lucy Long, are shown in this 1940s' photograph preparing cane for basketmaking, with the help of two small children. *Museum of the Cherokee Indian*

ABOVE: A group of young women learn to weave the traditional intricately patterned baskets produced by the Cherokee at the Cherokee Boarding School during the early 1950s. *Museum of the Cherokee Indian*

RIGHT: Although the dwelling is simple, a great deal of care has been taken by the Henry Reed family (of the late 1940s) to landscape their picturesque hillside home in North Carolina. *Museum of the Cherokee Indian*

RIGHT: Eagle wands, partially finished masks, a drum, pottery, fringed dresses, canes, carvings, and other assorted Cherokee handcrafts are shown in this undated still life. *Museum of the Cherokee Indian*

LEFT: An unidentified "chief" in costume demonstrates the use of a traditional blowgun, used for centuries by the Cherokee in their woodland home. *Museum of the Cherokee Indian*

ABOVE: A group of handwoven baskets sits atop boulders, with the Oconaluftee River in the background. The Cherokee have been known especially for their baskets and pottery.
Museum of the Cherokee Indian

ABOVE: Mary Shell, a Cherokee weaver, is shown "loose-warp" finger-weaving what appears to be a sash in this undated photo from the late 1940s. The frame is made from saplings. *Museum of the Cherokee Indian*

ABOVE: Cherokee Welcome League, 1967. The Cherokee were among the first Indians to adopt European-style clothing rather than traditional garb. Most Cherokee continue to dress in the style of average Americans of most any time period. *Museum of the Cherokee Indian*

ABOVE: Pottery of many different American Indian tribes has used effigies, that is to say stylized likenesses of animals. This oil lamp is formed in the likeness of a bird. *Museum of the Cherokee Indian*

ABOVE: An undated photo shows an old-style Cherokee wooden dugout canoe. Canoes of this type were hollowed out from single felled logs by alternately burning and using axes to remove excess wood. *Museum of the Cherokee Indian*

ABOVE: An undated 19th-century photograph shows numerous pottery vessels found at an excavation of an old Cherokee village. Styles include simple daily-use vessels and more ceremonial-type shaped pieces. *Museum of the Cherokee Indian*

Cherokee Ind n   ther - Ch   e N.C   I-P-134

ABOVE: An early 20th century picture postcard shows a Cherokee mother with a child and an infant in a sling on her back. Much of their clothing is made of simple cotton calico fabric. *Museum of the Cherokee Indian*

LEFT: A young David Lossiah inspects either a butterfly or dragonfly in this 1940s' photo. He is dressed in modern-day T-shirt and commercial overalls. *Museum of the Cherokee Indian*

ABOVE: An unusual mix of clothing styles is found in this late 1940s' image of Carl Standingdeer and troupe. Most members are wearing "traditional" tourist-style headdresses and costumes, but have modern-day pants with belts. *Museum of the Cherokee Indian*

ABOVE: This 1950s' photograph of the playground and surrounding area of the Cherokee School on the Qualla Boundary Indian Reservation could have been from most any other part of the country. Students are dressed in contemporary styles. *Museum of the Cherokee Indian*

ABOVE: Historical Association in Cherokee, *c.* 1940s. A group of individuals meeting as the Cherokee Historical Association was largely responsible for the planning and execution of the Museum of the Cherokee Indian and the extensive archives it preserves. *Museum of the Cherokee Indian*

ABOVE: Lottie Smith Patee (seen in the 1880s), of the Eastern Band of Cherokee, was an early graduate of the Hampton Normal & Agricultural Institute. The school attempted to "civilize" Indian students by removing their culture. *Museum of the Cherokee Indian*

ABOVE: Downtown Cherokee, N.C., 1949. During the late 1940s, the Eastern Band of Cherokee made a conscious decision to embrace the tourist trade for financial reasons. Their proximity to the Great Smoky Mountains made it highly successful. *Museum of the Cherokee Indian*

ABOVE: Cherokee, N.C., 1949. As a part of the expansion to embrace tourists, downtown Cherokee came alive with various curio and craft shops, gas stations, motels, jewelry stores, and the accompanying motor traffic. *Museum of the Cherokee Indian*

Recent History and Today

Oklahoma attained statehood in 1907, and tribal sovereignty was ended. The federal government appointed chiefs to the Cherokee Nation, often just long enough to sign a treaty. Many of these were known as "one-day chiefs." A general convention was convened by the Cherokee in 1938 to elect a chief. They choose J. B. Milam as principal chief and, as a goodwill gesture, President Franklin Delano Roosevelt confirmed the election in 1941.

W. W. Keeler, CEO of Phillips Petroleum, was appointed chief by Harry S. Truman in 1949. In 1971, he became the first elected chief of the tribe under the self-determination policy signed by President Richard Nixon. Chad Smith, who is currently the chief of the Nation, was re-elected in 2007.

The United Keetoowah Band took a different track than the Cherokee Nation, and received federal recognition after the Indian Reorganization Act of 1934. They are descended from the Old Settlers, the Cherokees who moved west before the forced removal. The tribe currently requires a quarter-blood percentage for enrollment. UKB members must descend from an ancestor who is listed on the Final Dawes Roll of the Cherokee. Thus, the descendant of a Cherokee living in Texas at the time of the Dawes Roll would be ineligible for enrollment now, regardless of bloodlines. The current chief of the UKB is George Wickliffe, who was inaugurated in 2005.

As for the Eastern Band, they continue to grow and develop under the leadership of Chief Michell Hicks, who was elected in 2003, and again in 2007. Among the many cultural resources of the Eastern Band is the Museum of the Cherokee Indian, which not only tells the history of the tribe effectively, but also has significant archival and genealogical records. Membership in the band requires one-sixteenth Cherokee blood and ancestral listing on the 1924 Baker Roll (a listing of the Eastern Band as it existed at that time).

Although there is now more communication between the three bands than there used to be, each still operates as an independent government, and there is more than a little friction between the Cherokee Nation and the UKB.

One of the biggest issues facing the western Cherokee bands is that of the tribal status of Cherokee Freedmen, descendants of black slaves owned by Cherokee Indians. The Freedmen were first guaranteed Cherokee citizenship via treaty in 1866, and this was reinforced by the Dawes Commission Land Rolls, but their citizenship was revoked by the Cherokee Nation in the 1980s in an effort to establish bloodline tribal membership. Although many Freedmen have some Cherokee blood, not all have enough to qualify for tribal membership. On March 7, 2006, the Cherokee Nation Judicial Appeal Tribunal announced a controversial ruling that the Cherokee Freedmen were eligible once again for citizenship, because it did not limit membership to people possessing Cherokee blood. This ruling was consistent with the 1975

OPPOSITE: The Cherokee Today. The territory now held by the Cherokee (all three bands) is only a very tiny percentage of the vast area of more than 40,000 square miles of their ancestral grounds.

THE CHEROKEE TODAY

There are only three federally recognized Cherokee groups with the Bureau of Indian Affairs (BIA) given as:

(1) Oklahoma Cherokee (Cherokee Nation) enrollment only requires proof of Western Cherokee ancestry–228,307

(2) United Keetoowah Band, a sub-group of (1), descendants or members of an old 19th century society in the southeastern part of the old Cherokee Nation who have reported themselves separately in recent census-7,953

(3) Eastern Cherokee of the Qualla Reservation in North Carolina who require 1/32nd Cherokee ancestry for enrollment-12,139

It is estimated between 40-50% of these members live within the borders of the old Cherokee Nation or the Qualla Reservation.

However, there are over 50 organizations in at least 12 states who lay claim to Cherokee descent, some of whom were reported in the self-identifying 2000 census.

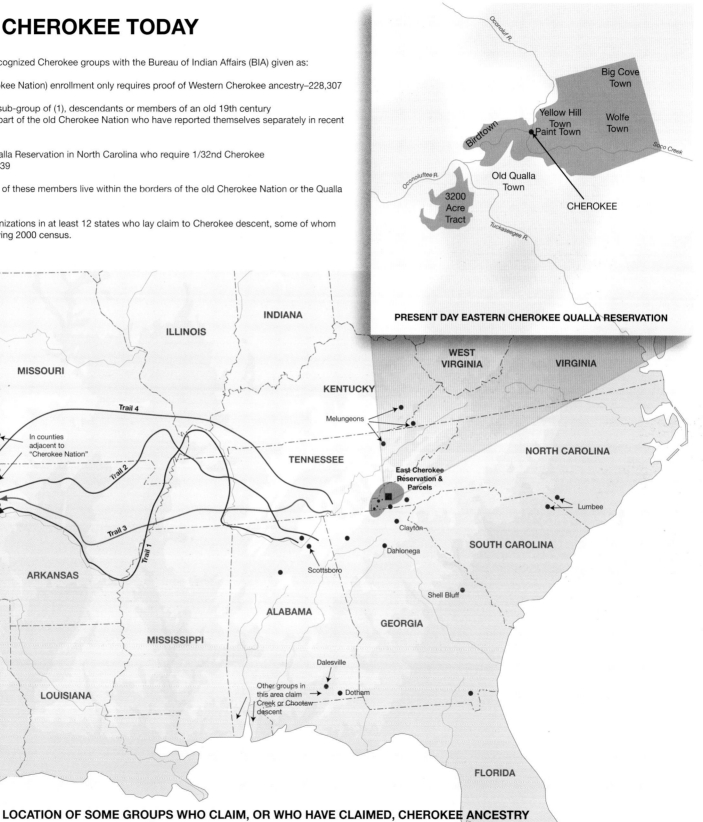

PRESENT DAY EASTERN CHEROKEE QUALLA RESERVATION

LOCATION OF SOME GROUPS WHO CLAIM, OR WHO HAVE CLAIMED, CHEROKEE ANCESTRY

RIGHT: Cherokee Female Seminary, Oklahoma. Seminary Hall was completed in 1889, and was built of locally produced materials. It replaced the original seminary building, which burned in 1887. It is the oldest institution of higher learning for women west of the Mississippi. *Library of Congress Prints and Photographs Division*

Constitution of the Cherokee Nation, which accepted Cherokee Freedmen on the basis of historical citizenship, rather than evidenced blood relation. Chief Smith later announced that the issue of Freedmen citizenship was being considered for a vote that would propose amendments to the Constitution. These amendments were intended to restrict tribal membership exclusively to Cherokees by blood descent, thus excluding the Freedmen. In March 2007, the tribe voted on the constitutional amendment, with more than three-fourths approving the exclusion. This vote to oust the Freedmen from the tribe provoked tremendous controversy, including pressure from the Congressional Black Caucus, which called for the revocation of all federal funding for the Cherokee Nation. The Cherokee Freedmen were reinstated as citizens of the Cherokee Nation by the Cherokee Nation Tribal Courts on May 15, 2007. The issue is not yet fully resolved, and black Congresswoman Diane Watson (D-Calif.) has introduced a bill that would sever ties between the United States and the Cherokee Nation until the Freedmen issue is resolved.

On a more positive note, the Cherokee Nation participates in numerous joint programs with the Eastern Band and takes part in cultural exchange programs and joint Tribal Council meetings that address issues affecting all Cherokee People.

LEFT: Part of the Pan-Indian movement, the annual Chehaw National Indian Festival is held at Chehaw Park in Albany, Georgia. This Cherokee man is wearing a headdress made of painted wood and feathers, and is preparing for a ceremonial dance.
Kevin Fleming/Corbis

OPPOSITE: On June 23, 1963, leaders of the Grand Council of the American Indian met for the first time since 1775. Although dressed in "dime store Indian" costume, they sought to bring together Indians as they were before the "artificial barriers of the white man." Among the Cherokee present was Frank Tompee-Saw (left).
Bettmann/Corbis

ABOVE: The Government Indian School near Cherokee, North Carolina, can be seen in this 1909 panoramic photograph. The school is nestled on a hillside near a river. The reservation is adjacent to the Great Smoky Mountains. *Library of Congress Prints and Photographs Division*

LEFT: Ruth Muskrat, a Cherokee, presents President Calvin Coolidge with a copy of a book entitled *The Red Man in the United States*, a work describing the status at that time of the American Indian. Photograph taken December 1923. *Library of Congress Prints and Photographs Division LC-USZ62-107775*

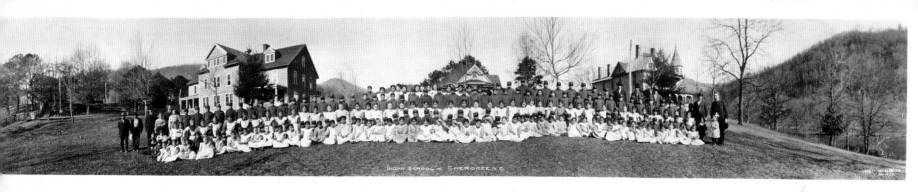

ABOVE: A panoramic hilltop view of the Indian School in Cherokee, North Carolina, shows a large number of male and female students, all in western dress. *c. 1909. Library of Congress Prints and Photographs Division LC-USZ62-122837*

RIGHT: Rosie the Riveter (Cherokee version). In this World War II patriotic photo, Petrina Moore, a full-blooded Cherokee, is shown (welding mask lifted) working as a welder at the Todd Hoboken dry dock in 1943. *Library of Congress Prints and Photographs Division LC-USW33-025830-C*

ABOVE: A patriotic photo taken during the approach to World War II in 1941 shows three Indian men in uniform. *Left to right:* Corporal Jesse McNevins, Cherokee; Corporal Tommy Hattensty, Choctaw; Sergeant Douglas Burris, Chickasaw. All three were members of Company H, 179th Infantry, Oklahoma National Guard. *Corbis*

LEFT: A Cherokee man in costume prepares for a ceremonial dance at the 1995 Chehaw National Indian Festival held in Chehaw Park, Albany, Georgia. His costume represents those of several tribes. *Kevin Fleming/Corbis*

ABOVE: A 1930 photo features an attractive young Oklahoma Cherokee woman, sitting on a stone in what was considered a traditional beaded, fringed dress that borrowed from several tribes. *Bettmann/Corbis*

RIGHT: A group of Cherokee dancers perform in "native dress" at the 1995 annual Chehaw National Indian Festival. *Kevin Fleming/Corbis*

ABOVE: A 1946 head and shoulders photo of Carl Standingdeer, of the Eastern Band of Cherokee. Standingdeer was one of many members who supported passage of a bill to limit tribal membership to those with more than one-sixteenth Cherokee blood. *Bettmann/Corbis*

LEFT: Chris Thacker, a young dancer, waits his turn to compete in a 1995 powwow dance competition, wearing a headdress made from feathers and horse hair. The Pan-Indian movement has spawned many powwows across the country. *Lindsay Hebberd/Corbis*

RIGHT: A Cherokee Indian is dressed in an elaborate costume during the 1999 Miccosukee Tribe Arts Festival. Among other things he is wearing a roach, beaded headband, and bone-bead breastplate.
Tony Arruza/Corbis

OPPOSITE: President John F. Kennedy met with representatives of 90 Indian tribes on August 15, 1962, and was presented with the Declaration of Indian Purpose. Kennedy stated that "All Americans have a strong obligation to improve the living conditions of the Indians." Eleanor Red Fawn Smooth (*left*), represented the Mohawk-Cherokee.
Bettmann/Corbis

RIGHT: A Cherokee woman demonstrates the art of finger weaving wool into ceremonial sashes at the Oconaluftee Indian Village, about 1955. The village is a working replica of an 18th century community.

RIGHT: Cherokee dance from "Unto These Hills." Cherokee members dance during an outdoor presentation of Cherokee history in the village of Cherokee, North Carolina. The outdoor drama is produced by both the Eastern Band and the Cherokee Nation in Oklahoma. From a c. 1955 postcard. *W. M. Cline Co., Chattanooga, Tennessee*

LEFT: The Mountainside Theatre, where the drama "Unto These Hills" is performed during the summer months. The close-by Museum of the Cherokee Indian and Oconaluftee Indian Village also give details of historic Cherokee life. *W. M. Cline Co., Chattanooga, Tennessee*

LEFT: A scene from the outdoor drama "Unto These Hills" showing the Cherokee assembled for the journey into exile in Indian Territory (now Oklahoma). Cherokee descendants participate each summer in the drama at the Mountainside Theatre. From a *c.* 1956 postcard. *W. M. Cline Co., Chattanooga, Tennessee*

ABOVE: A group of young Cherokee men from the Qualla Boundary Reservation practice their archery skills in the 1940s. They are identified as (*left to right*) Dick Driver, Boyd Catolster, and Johnson Catolster. *Museum of the Cherokee Indian*

ABOVE: A group of young women also practice their archery skills at the Cherokee Training School in the 1940s. They are identified as (*left to right*) Betty Catolster, Sally Crowe, and Sarah Wayne. *Museum of the Cherokee Indian*

ABOVE: A group of mostly World War I Eastern Band Cherokee veterans from American Legion Post 143, posing in 1938. Cherokee Indians have fought as Americans in every war since the Civil War. *Museum of the Cherokee Indian*

RIGHT: By the mid-20th century, the Cherokee Training School on the Qualla Boundary Reservation was teaching traditional skills, but with more modern technology. A weaving class uses modern looms. *Museum of the Cherokee Indian*

Leaders and Warriors

As is so often the case in any culture, few notable Cherokee people—past or present—sought to become important. Most were thrust into circumstances beyond their control and emerged as leaders. The Cherokee count many notable people among their number. Some are important to the Cherokee specifically; others had a larger role in shaping history or culture.

From an Indian point of view, by far the most significant figures to the Cherokee are First Man (*Kanati*, the great hunter) and First Woman (*Selu*, the corn bearer) From these two mythical figures emerged all Cherokee people.

Arguably, however, the two most vital historical figures in the development and survival of the Cherokee as we know them, are Sequoyah, who developed the Cherokee syllabary, or alphabet, and John Ross, the first elected principal chief of the tribe, who steered his people through the Trail of Tears, the establishment of a new nation, and the Civil War, all of which divided the tribe.

Other important, if not controversial, Cherokee figures include Nancy Ward, who was considered both a skillful warrior and an effective leader. She took an active role in negotiating the Hopewell Treaty in 1785, along with Corn Tassel, who also was a strong leader.

Not all notable Cherokee have an honored place in Cherokee history. Major Ridge is known mostly as a figure of betrayal as a member of the Treaty Party who signed the 1835 Treaty of New Echota, which led directly to the Trail of Tears. Others in the Treaty Party include Elias Boudinot (first editor of the *Cherokee Phoenix* newspaper), Ridge's son John, and Stand Watie, who became a Confederate general. Both Ridge and Boudinot were murdered for their actions, but Watie was warned in time and escaped.

Half-brother to Elias Boudinot, Watie became an important figure in the development of the Cherokee Nation. Other famous or important Cherokee in the years since include Ned Christie, a Cherokee patriot who became the subject of many books and magazine articles, including *Ned Christie's War*, by noted author Robert J. Conley. Conley, who is Cherokee, has also written an important book on the history of the Cherokee, *The Cherokee Nation*.

Will Rogers is perhaps the most well-known of all Cherokee. Guitarist Jimi Hendrix was Cherokee through his maternal grandmother, Nora Rose Moore, and legend has it that Elvis Presley was part Cherokee. Businessman and owner of the Tennessee Titans football team, Bud Adams, is an enrolled member of the tribe.

Other famous people of at least partial Cherokee ancestry include actors Johnny Depp, James Garner, James Earl Jones, Chuck Norris, Burt Reynolds, and Wes Studi. Musicians Eartha Kitt and Jonas Brothers, as well as painter Robert Rauschenberg and writer Mitch Cullin also all claim Cherokee heritage.

LEFT: Tooan Tuh or Dustu, "Spring Frog." From a lithograph, artist unknown in McKenney and Hall, c. 1836. Spring Frog was born near Lookout Mountain, Georgia, about 1754. He was reported to be an excellent hunter and ball-player. He fought with the Americans at Horseshoe Bend and was one of the earliest "Old Settlers" to Arkansas. *Author's collection*

RIGHT: Cunne Shote or Stalking Turkey. Colored engraving by Pierre Duflos (1742–1816). He, Ostenaco, and Pouting Pigeon were the "Three Chiefs" who visited England in 1762 and were painted by Sir Joshua Reynolds. *c.* 1780. *Private Collection/Stapleton Collection/ Bridgeman Art Library*

SE-QUO-YAH.

Philadelphia Published by Key & Biddle.

LEFT: Sequoyah or George Guess (or Gist). This portrait from an 1834 lithograph is based on a well-known painting by George Bird King of 1828. Sequoyah's syllabary is responsible for the Cherokee Nation becoming literate "almost overnight." He died in 1843, and the massive trees of California (*Sequoia gigantea*) are named in his honor. *Library of Congress Prints and Photographs Division LC-USZC4-4815*

RIGHT: Tahchee or Tatsi, known as "Captain Dutch." From McKenney & Hall's *The Indian Tribes of North America*. Tahchee was born about 1790. Foreseeing disastrous results of white contact, he and his followers emigrated west long before the main removal in 1838–39. George Catlin also sketched him in 1834. *Library of Congress Prints and Photographs Division LC-USZC4-12427*

OPPOSITE: Major General Winfield Scott. Engraving by William G. Armstrong (1823–90) after a portrait by Charles Cromwell Ingham (1796–1863). General Scott (1786–1866) was one of the few involved with the forced removal of the Cherokee who felt they should be treated with dignity and respect. By and large his orders were disregarded. *Private Collection/ Stapleton Collection/ Bridgeman Art Library*

A. Newsam

TAH-CHEE

A. CHEROKEE CHIEF

Philadelphia Published by E.C.Biddle

Entered according to act of Congress in the year 1837 by E.C. Biddle in the Clerks Office of the District Court of the Eastern District of Pa

RIGHT: David Vann. A Cherokee chief. Print c. 1843, from McKenney and Hall, published by Daniel Rice and James G. Clark. In 1801, David Vann, "a prominent mixed-blood chief," invited Moravians to establish the first mission in Cherokee territory. The mission became known as Spring Place. *Library of Congress Prints and Photographs Division LC-USZC4-12424*

DAVID VANN.

A CHEROKEE CHIEF.

PUBLISHED BY DANIEL RICE & JAMES G. CLARK, PHILAD.ª

Drawn, Printed & Col.ª at the Lithographic & Print Colouring Establishment. N.º 94 Walnut St Phila

Entered according to act of Congress in the Year 1843, by James G. Clark, in the Clerks office of the District Court of the Eastern District of Pennsylª

LEFT: Swimmer, or Ayunini, served in the Confederate Army in Company A, 69th North Carolina Infantry. He was proud of his ancient culture, and was a keeper of tradition, songs, and sacred formulae.

ABOVE: John Ridge, son of Major Ridge, was already a noted statesman when he joined his father and others who signed the Treaty of New Echota. He paid for that signature with his life. McKenney & Hall. *Library of Congress Prints and Photographs Division LC-USZC4-3157*

ABOVE: George (Major) Lowrey. George Lowrey was also known as Agili "He is Rising." He was a cousin of Sequoyah and assistant Chief of the Cherokee Nation in the West, about 1840. Painting attributed to John Mix Stanley, 1844.

LEFT: John Ross was the first elected principal chief of the Cherokee (1828–66), leading his people through the Trail of Tears and the Civil War. He was chief for 38 years. *Private Collection/Peter Newark American Pictures/ Bridgeman Art Library*

RIGHT: Col-Lee or Jol-Lee. Jol-Lee was a mixed-blood Western Cherokee band chief painted by George Catlin at Fort Gibson, Indian Territory, in 1834. He was likely the "Chief Jolly" who adopted the later famous Sam Houston, who took Talihina, Jolly's niece, as his second wife.

LEFT: Colonel E. C. Boudinot. Elias Cornelius Boudinot was the son of the first editor of the *Cherokee Phoenix* and, like his assassinated father, was a controversial figure among the Cherokee of his time. He was a colonel in the Confederate Army during the Civil War and subsequently was much involved in opening up the Indian Territory to white settlers and the railroads. *Library of Congress Prints and Photographs Division LC-BH83-968*

ABOVE: Walini was a Cherokee woman, probably Eastern Cherokee, who was photographed by James Mooney in 1888. Mooney's work, *Myths of the Cherokee*, published in 1900, remains a major source of information on the nation, although most material was from the Eastern Cherokee.

RIGHT: Sawanugi was an Eastern Cherokee photographed by James Mooney in 1888. The Ball Game is still played in Oklahoma and North Carolina and is somewhat similar to lacrosse.

LEFT: Chief Nimrod Jarrett Smith or Tsaladihi. Tsaladihi was son of a mixed-blood father and Indian mother. He was one of the many Cherokee who fought in the Confederate Army during the Civil War, and was principal chief of the Eastern Cherokee.

RIGHT: Iron Eyes Cody and Nancy Kwan. Iron Eyes Cody, who was not Indian but claimed Cherokee heritage, places a headdress on Nancy Kwan, known to movie-goers as "Suzie Wong." She was inducted into the Cherokee tribe in 1961 as an honorary member. *Bettmann/Corbis*

LEFT: Chief Wilma Mankiller. This portrait of Wilma Mankiller was taken in 2000, while she was principal chief of the Cherokee Nation in Oklahoma. Mankiller was the first female principal chief, first appointed to fulfill a term, then elected. *Buddy Mays/Corbis*

JOHN ROSS
1790 – 1866
PRINCIPAL CHIEF
OF THE
CHEROKEE NATION
1828 – 1866

LOYAL TO THE CHEROKEE
PEOPLE THRU FIVE
DECADES OF PUBLIC SERVICE

LEFT: Richard Taylor, 1788–1853, assistant principal chief of the Cherokee nation, 1851–53. *Library of Congress Prints and Photographs Division LC-USZ62-109119*

OPPOSITE: In this 1940s' photograph Carl Standingdeer is shown preparing to launch an arrow. Standingdeer is thought to have become the "most photographed man in America," due to his willingness to pose constantly for and with tourists. *Museum of the Cherokee Indian*

ABOVE: Samuel Austin Worcester, a white man, devoted his life to translating the Bible and hymns into the Cherokee language. He was also instrumental in setting up a printing press at Union Mission (Georgia) in 1835. *Museum of the Cherokee Indian*

ABOVE: William Holland Thomas. Will Thomas was a white trader who was raised by the Cherokee and spoke their language. It was partly through his efforts that the Eastern Band was officially established. He helped find and organize those in hiding, and helped others with citizenship. *Museum of the Cherokee Indian*

ABOVE: Rev. Jesse Bushyhead was in charge of the third group of Cherokee relocated in 1838–39. Of 950 who started, 898 arrived in Oklahoma, one of the higher rates of survival. This is surprising, since Bushyhead wrote that he had many "extremely aged and infirm" tribal members.

ABOVE: Joseph Vann. When Major Ridge introduced a resolution in 1832 to send a delegation to Washington City to discuss relocation with President Jackson (a resolution which was rejected by John Ross), Joseph Vann was among those selected as an alternative delegation. *Museum of the Cherokee Indian*

RIGHT: Although he was not a chief when he wrestled under the name "Chief Saunooke," Osley Bird Saunooke became principal chief of the Eastern Band of Cherokee in 1951. *Museum of the Cherokee Indian*

LEFT: Ella Mae Sequoyah walks along a street with her children in Cherokee, North Carolina, during the late 1940s. She carries her youngest in a back sling. The boy is barefoot.
Museum of the Cherokee Indian

RIGHT: This man, called Del, from an undated photograph of the late 19th century, was thought to have descended from a long line of Cherokee medicine men. *Museum of the Cherokee Indian*

LEFT: Anthropologist James Mooney, who wrote *The History, Myths and Sacred Formulas of the Cherokees* after spending time with the Eastern Band, identified this man as "Chief of the Coffin Makers. c. 1926–27." *Museum of the Cherokee Indian*

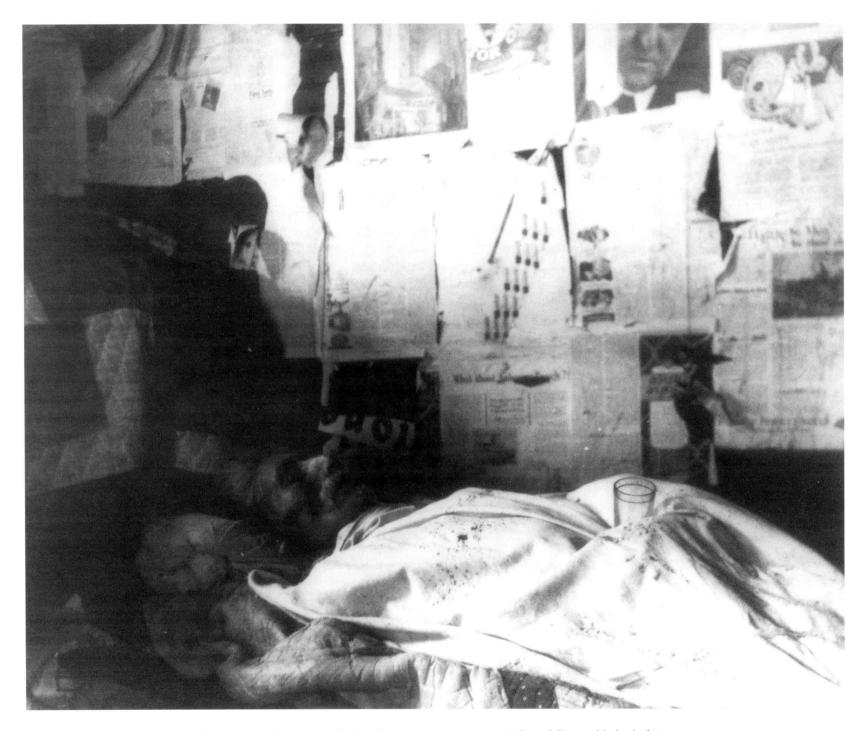

ABOVE: A Cherokee man called Og (Oganastota or Morgan Calhoun) lies on his bed after dying in 1926–27. Newspaper clippings line his walls. His wife was identified by the Smithsonian Institute as a medicine woman. *Museum of the Cherokee Indian*

LEFT: An unidentified family stands in a field near their North Carolina home in this early 20th century photo. The man appears Indian, but his wife seems to be white. Intermarriage was common in the Cherokee tribe. *Museum of the Cherokee Indian*

RIGHT: A Cherokee man is shown in this 1926–27 photo by Smithsonian photographer Franz Olbrechts, collecting the root of an "inverted raspberry branch" for use as medicine. *Museum of the Cherokee Indian*

Timeline

c. 1000: The Cherokee are known to have lived in the Tennessee River and Great Smoky Mountain areas.

1540: Spanish explorer Hernando De Soto and his gold-seeking party are the first whites known to have been seen by the Cherokee. De Soto writes about the "red men," who, he reports, have skin in a wide range of shades from "negro" to "fair." See map pages 36–37.

1629: The first traders from English settlements begin trading with the Cherokee people.

1721: The treaty with the Governor of the Carolinas is thought to be the first concession of land to the whites by the Cherokee.

1728: The first of three devastating smallpox epidemics hits the Cherokee.

1730: Cherokee leaders visit England (?)

1738: A smallpox epidemic eradicates 25 percent of the Cherokee Nation. Nancy Ward born.

1753: A third smallpox epidemic within 25 years sweeps through the Cherokee. Estimates are that half the pre-smallpox population has been wiped out by this point.

1755: Battle of Taliwa (numerous other spellings). Accounts differ on the exact events. However, the Creek, who greatly outnumber the Cherokee, attack the Cherokee line five times. During the fifth attack, elderly Cherokee leader Kingfisher is slain. His teenage wife, Nancy Ward, picks up his weapon and, chanting a Cherokee war song, leads the Cherokee to victory, routing the Creek. The battle marks the successful expulsion of the Creek from much of what is now north Georgia.

1756–63: The Cherokee fight in the French and Indian War allied with the British.

1771: Sequoyah born.

1776–83: Impressed by British conduct during the French and Indian War, the Cherokee side with them during the American Revolution.

1783: North Carolina grants land formerly belonging to the Cherokee to its citizens; the Cherokee cede land to Georgia.

1785–86: The Treaty of Hopewell is signed. It is the first treaty between the United States and the Cherokee. The Cherokee think this will be the end of the settlers' invasion of Cherokee land but within three years bitter fighting has erupted as settlers continue to move into the Cherokee Nation. This treaty is the basis for the term "Talking Leaves," the name of the tribe's written language. The Cherokee compare the written words with leaves. When they are no longer of use they wither and die.

1790: John Ross, first elected chief of the Cherokee, born.

1791: Treaty of Holston is signed. It calls for the United States to advance civilization of the Cherokee by giving them farm tools and technical advice. It also forces the Cherokee to cede land in eastern Tennessee in exchange for President Washington's guarantee that the Cherokee Nation will never again be invaded by settlers. This treaty requires Americans to obtain passports to enter Cherokee lands, and grants Cherokee the right to evict settlers. William Augustus Bowles and other Cherokee leaders visit England.

1796: George Washington begins "civilization" program among the Cherokee.

1799: The Lighthorse, a loose-knit Cherokee police force, is formed. It is headed by The Ridge and James Vann.

1802: Thomas Jefferson signs the Georgia Compact, allowing the state of Georgia to remove all Indians in exchange for abandonment of the state's claim to western lands.

1811: The New Madrid earthquake (actually three quakes) is felt throughout the Midwest. For the Cherokee Nation the quakes spark what is best described as a religious revival. Writer James Mooney later calls this movement the "Ghost Dance," after the similar Western Indian revival.

1813–14: Cherokee warriors fight alongside future president Andrew Jackson during two campaigns (five major battles) of the Creek War against the Red Stick Creeks, saving both his army and his life in separate battles.

1814: Cherokee "friend" Andrew Jackson demands cessions of 2.2 million acres from the Cherokee.

1817: The Cherokee adopt articles of government that give only the National Council the authority to cede Cherokee land. A treaty exchanges some tribal territory for land in Arkansas. Old Settlers begin voluntary migration and establish a government there.

1821: Sequoyah completes his Cherokee Syllabary. Within six months more than 25 percent of the Cherokee people learn how to read and write, leading to an eventual almost complete literacy rate among the Cherokees.

1822: The Cherokee Supreme Court is established.

1824: First written law of Western Cherokees takes effect.

1825: New Echota, Georgia, is authorized as the Cherokee capital.

1827: The modern Cherokee Nation begins, with the Cherokee Constitution established by a convention. The Constitution, based on the U.S. Constitution, provides for national sovereignty, as well as judicial, legislative, and executive branches of government.

1828: John Ross becomes the first elected chief, serving for 38 years, the longest reign of any Cherokee chief. The *Cherokee Phoenix* newspaper is established (Feb. 28). It is published in English and Cherokee. Andrew Jackson is elected President of the United States. Gold is discovered in Georgia, leading to a gold rush. The Arkansas Cherokee relocate to Indian Territory (Oklahoma).

1828–30: The Georgia Legislature abolishes tribal government and expands its authority over Cherokee country.

1830: Indian Removal Act is signed into federal law. This will eventually force many Indians to leave their homelands and move west.

1831: The U.S. Supreme Court declares the Cherokee Nation a "domestic dependent nation."

1832: U.S. Supreme Court decision, *Worcester vs. Georgia*, establishes tribal sovereignty in Georgia and protects Cherokees from Georgia laws. President Jackson, however, does not enforce the decision and Georgia holds a lottery for Cherokee lands.

1835: Treaty Party, including *Cherokee Phoenix* founder Elias Boudinot, signs the Treaty of New Echota (Dec. 29), giving up title to all Cherokee lands in the southeast in exchange for land in Indian Territory.

1836: The U.S. Senate ratifies the Treaty of New Echota.

1838–39: Trail of Tears. U.S. Government's forced removal of at least 16,000 Cherokees and their slaves in defiance of Supreme Court decision. More than 4,000 Cherokee die from exposure and disease along the way.

1839: Treaty Party leaders Major Ridge, John Ridge, and Elias Boudinot are assassinated for breaking pact not to sign the Treaty of New Echota. Factionalism continues until 1846. A new Constitution is ratified at a convention uniting Cherokees arriving from the east with those in the west.

1844: The Cherokee Supreme Court building opens. The *Cherokee Advocate* becomes the first newspaper in Indian Territory.

1846: The U.S. Government recognizes the Western Cherokee as the owners of their land in Indian Territory.

1851: Cherokee male and female seminaries are opened by the Cherokee. The female seminary is the first secondary school for girls west of the Mississippi.

1859: Original Keetoowah Society is organized to maintain traditions and to fight slavery.

1860: Tension mounts between Union Cherokees and Confederate Cherokees.

1861: Cherokee Nation allies with the Confederate Government. The Cherokee Nation will be torn by border warfare throughout the Civil War.

1865–66: Cherokee Nation negotiates peace with the U.S. Government and is forced to give up much land in Oklahoma supposedly because of actions in the war. New treaty limits tribal land

rights and eliminates the possibility of a Cherokee state. This treaty is a prelude to the Dawes Commission. John Ross dies.

1887: General Allotment Act passed. The act requires individual ownership of lands once held in common by Indian tribes.

1889: The Qualla Reservation of the Eastern Band of Cherokees in North Carolina is formed. Unassigned land in Indian Territory is opened by white settlers known as "boomers."

1890: The Oklahoma Territory is organized out of the western half of Indian Territory.

1893: The so-called Cherokee Strip opened to white settlers. Dawes Commission arrives.

1898: The Curtis Act is passed, abolishing tribal courts.

1903: William C. Rogers becomes the last elected Cherokee chief for 69 years.

1905: Land allotment begins after official Dawes roll is taken of Cherokees.

1907: Oklahoma statehood combines Indian and Oklahoma Territories and dissolves the Cherokee tribal government.

1917: William C. Rogers, the last elected Cherokee chief, dies.

1934: Indian Reorganization Act establishes a land base for tribes and legal structure for self-government.

1948: Chief J. B. Milam calls Cherokee Convention. This is the beginning of a model tribal government of the Cherokee Nation.

1949: W. W. Bill Keeler is last appointed Cherokee chief. Keeler, appointed by President Truman, was a part-time chief and was Chief Executive Officer of Phillips Petroleum. He becomes first elected chief in 69 years in 1971.

1957: First Cherokee National Holiday (held annually on Labor Day weekend).

1961: Cherokees are awarded $15 million by the U.S. Claims Commission for Cherokee Strip lands.

1963: The Cherokee National Historical Society is founded. CNHS opens Ancient Village in 1967, begins Trail of Tears drama in 1969 and opens museum in 1975.

1967: The Cherokee Foundation is formed to purchase land on which the tribal complex now sits.

1970: A U.S. Supreme Court ruling confirms Cherokee Nation ownership of the river bed and banks of 96-mile segment of the Arkansas River.

1971: W. W. Keeler becomes first elected principal chief since 1903. He has served (unelected) since his appointment by President Truman in 1949.

1975: Ross O. Swimmer is elected to first of three terms as principal chief. First Cherokee Tribal Council elected. Congress passes Indian Self-Determination and Education Assistance Acts.

1976: Cherokee voters ratify a new Constitution outlining tribal government.

1979: Tribal offices are moved into a new modern complex south of Tahlequah.

1984: A joint council meeting between Eastern Band of Cherokees and Cherokee Nation is held at Red Clay, Tennessee. It is the first such meeting in 146 years. Council meetings are now held bi-annually.

1985: Upon the resignation of Ross Swimmer as chief, Wilma Mankiller fulfills remaining term, becoming first woman Cherokee chief.

1987: Wilma Mankiller makes history and draws international attention to tribe as the first woman elected chief of the Cherokee Nation. Cherokee voters pass constitution amendment to elect council by districts in 1991.

1988: Cherokee Nation joins Eastern Band in Cherokee, N.C., to commemorate the 150th anniversary of the beginning of the Trail of Tears.

1989: The Cherokee Nation observes 150th anniversary of arrival in Indian Territory, "A New Beginning."

1990: Chief Mankiller signs the historic self-governance agreement, making the Cherokee Nation one of six tribes to participate in the self-determination project. The project, which will run for three years, beginning October 1, 1990, authorizes the tribe to assume tribal responsibility for Bureau of Indian Affairs funds, which were formerly being spent on the tribe's behalf at the agency, area, and central office levels.

1991: The July tribal election marks the first council to be elected by districts since statehood, and Wilma Mankiller wins her second elected term as principal chief with a landslide 82 percent of the votes cast.

1995: Joe Byrd becomes principal chief of the Cherokee, marking the first time in almost 200 years that full-blood bilingual leaders occupy the top positions of the Cherokee Nation. (Byrd was not actually elected. His name appeared on a runoff ballot with George Bearpaw and the Judicial Appeals Tribunal ordered that no votes for Bearpaw would be counted, leaving Byrd to become chief by default.)

1999: Chad Smith (Corntassel) is elected as principal chief, defeating Byrd. He continues to serve at the time of writing, having been re-elected in 2003 and again in 2007.

Bibliography

Birchfield, D. L., *Cherokee*. Milwaukee, WI: Gareth Stevens Publishing, 2004.

Byers, Ann, *The Trail of Tears: A Primary Source History of the Forced Relocation of the Cherokee Nation*. New York: The Rosen Publishing Group, 2004.

Conley, Robert J., *The Cherokee Nation: A History*. Albuquerque: University of New Mexico Press, 2005.

Englar, Mary, *The Cherokee and Their History*. Minneapolis, MN: Compass Point Books, 2006.

Johnson, Michael: *Encyclopedia of Native Tribes of North America*. Third edition, London: Compendium Publishing, 2007.

King, Duane H., ed., *The Cherokee Indian Nation: A Troubled History*. Knoxville, TN: The University of Tennessee Press, 1979.

Levine, Michelle, *The Cherokees*. Minneapolis, MN: Lerner Publications, 2007.

Mooney, James, *James Mooney's History, Myths, and Sacred Formulas of the Cherokees*. Asheville, NC: Bright Mountain Books, 1992.

Peithmann, Irvin M., *Red Men of Fire: A History of the Cherokee Indian*. Springfield, IL: Charles C. Thomas, 1964.

Perdue, Theda and Michael D. Green, *The Cherokee Nation and the Trail of Tears*. New York: Viking Penguin, 2007.

——, *The Cherokee Removal: A Brief History with Documents*. Boston: Bedford Books/St. Martin's Press, 1995.

Rozema, Vicki, ed., *Voices From The Trail of Tears*. Winston-Salem, NC: John F. Blair, 2003.

Stewart, Philip, *Cherokee*. Broomall, PA: Mason Crest Publishers, 2004.

Woodward, Grace Steele, *The Cherokees*. Norman, OK: University of Oklahoma Press, 1963.